THE PUZZLE OF GOD

Comments on *Puzzle of God*

This book is a masterpiece of coherence. Step by step the reader is led clearly and humorously through the philosophical maze which confuses our thinking about God.

This will be an invaluable resource for sixth form Philosophy of Religion teachers and students, and many an undergraduate will discover it with much relief!

Linda Smith
Head of Department of Religious Education
King's College, London

PETER VARDY

The Puzzle of God

Collins
FLAME

HarperCollins*Religious*
Part of HarperCollins*Publishers*
77–85 Fulham Palace Road, London W6 8JB

First published in Great Britain
in 1990 by Flame

3 5 7 9 10 8 6 4

A catalogue record for this book is
available from the British Library

ISBN 000 599223 0

Printed and bound in Great Britain by
HarperCollinsManufacturing Glasgow

To my wife, Anne
– again

With thanks for enduring patience, tolerance, support, love –
and five children!

Amor vincit omnia

CONTENTS

LETTER TO THE READER

Dear Reader

Poets, musicians, philosophers and saints have, throughout the centuries, sought to communicate the reality of God to the world. Today we live in a rational age and their voices are muted. Still the eternal questions remain to challenge us and to mock the shortness of our brief lives.

In this book I have tried to present, clearly and simply, the main features of many of the central debates concerning God's reality and how God is to be understood. No answers are given – rather the aim is to help you, the reader, to think through the problems for yourself. Wherever specialised terms are used, they are defined so that no previous knowledge or reading is required.

The search for truth is never a comfortable one. It is always easier and more secure not to think and to remain content with our own certainties. Yet, whether we are believers or non-believers, doubts and problems about our own positions creep into our minds, however much we may try to avoid thinking about them. If there is a creator God, surely He has created our minds, and so the search for truth should not lead us away from Him. If there is no creator God, we have only ourselves on whom to depend. The search for truth and meaning is one of the few things that endure in a transitory world. As the book of Proverbs says when talking about wisdom:

Receive my instruction and not silver;
and knowledge rather than choice gold.
For wisdom is better than rubies;
and all the things that may be desired are not to be compared
to it.

(Proverbs 8:10–11)

This book is a small attempt to help in the search for understanding. It is a search that will never be completely achieved, but this does not mean that the attempt must not be made. I hope you find the quest as exciting and worthwhile as I do.

My thanks are due to my wife Anne for her great patience in commenting on the draft manuscript and for her help in proof-reading. I am also grateful to Philip Gudgeon SJ, Sarah Allen and Gwyneth Little for their comments. Also I owe a real debt to the undergraduate and postgraduate students at Heythrop College, the smallest College of London University, where I lecture. I am also indebted to those studying for the Masters degree in the philosophy of religion at the Institute of Education, London. Their open-minded search for truth as well as their friendship have meant and still mean a great deal to me.

Peter Vardy
St. Clair
Devon.

Heythrop College
University of London
Advent 1989 to Epiphany 1990

ONE

Unicorns, Numbers and God

1. (a) I believe in God.
   (b) I do not believe in God.

2. (a) I believe in unicorns.
   (b) I do not believe in unicorns.

We all know what a unicorn is. If we met one walking down our local High Street we would recognise it. We might, of course, have some doubts as to whether it was a real unicorn. We might well suspect that it was a trick of some sort, and might imagine that what we saw was a horse which had had a spiral horn somehow grafted onto its forehead. However, there would be tests that we could apply, and these might well include finding out where the animal came from. It may well be that we think that meeting a unicorn is so unlikely that no tests would satisfy us – in this case we would be sceptical about the possibility of unicorns. We would agree about what a unicorn would be like – but we would simply deny that there were such animals!

Imagine that you have a friend who is useless at mathematics. As soon as he sees a mathematical symbol, his mind goes blank. He has no notion of the basic elements of mathematics, although he is otherwise intelligent. Imagine that you try to explain to him what a prime number is. You might say: "A prime number is any whole number that is divisible by itself and one and by no other number." You might go on to give examples and to tell him that the numbers 2, 3, 5, 7, 11, 13, 17, 19 and so on are prime numbers and that there are an infinite number of prime numbers. The person to whom you are explaining might, however, not be able to make anything of all this talk – to him, prime numbers are simply not real. They are a curious idea used by mathematicians, but they are simply irrelevant and make no sense to him. Finally he might say to you: "You say prime numbers are real and that they exist. All right – show me one." You will probably be puzzled by this – you can't put him in a car and drive him to see the prime number 17. Prime numbers certainly exist, but you cannot go to visit them. The prime number 17, or any other prime number, is not sitting in a particular place. The very fact that he asks you to show him a prime number means that he has not understood what a prime number is.

We understand what unicorns are and most of us accept that they do not exist. We understand what prime numbers are and most of us accept that prime numbers exist – albeit in a different way to unicorns. We understand that trees, love, atoms and evil exist – but in different ways. What, however, does it mean to talk of God existing?

The word God has been the most fought-over and debated word in the history of ideas. For centuries it dominated the thought of the most intelligent people on this planet. Even today, talk about God is guaranteed to raise the passions. Religion is an emotive subject, and around the world families and communities are divided from each other because of different religious beliefs. All too often these beliefs are passionately held, yet all too rarely do those holding the beliefs stop to think about what it is that they believe.

Even within a particular community people will differ about what the word God means. Many people have a somewhat childish idea of God, seeing Him as an old man with a white beard sitting somewhere above the clouds. If we talk to someone else about God, we will normally find considerable differences between the two of us, and examining these differences with an open mind can help each of us to be clear about what we do and do not believe.

Philosophy is partly concerned with a search for truth and understanding. In this book we will be taking this search seriously. There is no hidden agenda, no attempt to provide you with the "right" answer. Rather, the aim is to help you, the reader, to think through what God means and then to go on to explore the consequences of holding this view. Whatever view you hold is going to be fraught with difficulties and complications. Some people are nervous of philosophy because they do not think it is right to think about or to examine their faith. However, most religions make a claim to truth, and so this claim should be taken seriously. Any religion that seeks truth should not be frightened of the search for greater understanding. Samuel Taylor Coleridge put it this way:

He who begins by loving Christianity better than truth will proceed by loving his own sect or Church better than Christianity and end by loving himself better than all.

If we refuse to seek the truth, if we retreat behind our own certainties because we are frightened that they cannot bear examination, then we are likely to become increasingly intolerant of others. In a world where there are many different religious systems, the search for truth and understanding must be a worthy one. In previous centuries, religious wars were used by one religious grouping to impose their beliefs on others. We should have moved beyond that stage now (although events such as the condemnation to death of the author Salman Rushdie make us ask whether we have), and we should be able to sit down with friends who have different religious beliefs and reason our way towards greater mutual understanding.

In the pages that follow we shall look at four different ideas of what it means to talk about God. All these ideas are persuasive, all are influential. Some have an ancient history, others have their roots in the past but have been more recently brought up to date. All are credible, all suffer from disadvantages. In exploring these different ideas of God we will be exploring the very heart of religion and, by so doing, we may be able to come closer to the goal of our own search for ultimate truth.

[handwritten annotation: Nowhere in this chapter is there any mention of any atheistic belief & yet the author tells us he seeks the truth.]

TWO

What is Truth?

[handwritten margin note: It is not a method any rational person (would advocate)]

One way of learning to swim is to be thrown into the deep end! We are going straight into a discussion which is probably going to be at the heart of philosophy and theology in the next century, yet few people are aware of the issues. It really revolves around the question that Pontius Pilate asked Jesus – "What is truth?" This is tremendously important – particularly when we start to consider what it means to say that a religious or a moral claim is true.

To understand the issues, we are going to have to think about how language is used. We learn language at our parents' knees. Very young children have an innate ability to master language. This mastery is one of the key elements in human development. Early man developed an ability to wield tools, but as the first inarticulate grunts developed into a means of communication, so it became possible for individuals to co-operate towards some common end. Language is a public affair. It is the way in which we communicate ideas, aspirations, truths, objectives and insights. We use language to tell others of our needs, feelings and intentions.

Language is not static – it is developing all the time. New words are introduced and the meanings of old words change. The meaning of the term, a "gay young man" a hundred years ago was entirely different to what it is today. Even thirty years ago, a billion in Britain meant a million million. Today Britain has adopted the United States convention and a billion means a thousand million – a substantial difference. Terms

like nuclear disarmament, embryo research, charged part-
icles, acid rain or video recorder simply did not exist until
recently, as the ideas they represented were not there to be
expressed.

Language is rich and it is dynamic. It expresses truth – and,
of course, it can also express falsity. However, what does it
mean for language to express truth? Take a simple statement
like: "Murder is wrong." What does it mean to say that this
statement is true? Most people would probably agree with
this view, but that does not mean that we understand
what would be necessary to make the statement true.

There are two basic theories of truth, or ways of understanding truth:

The correspondence theory of truth

The correspondence theory of truth maintains that a statement is true if it corresponds to a state of affairs which is
independent of language and of the society in which we live.
Someone who holds to a correspondence theory of truth is
today called a *realist*.

Realists maintain that reality is separate from our language
and that our language stretches out to a reality that is external
to us and tries to express it accurately. Sometimes we make
errors – for instance, people once believed that the world was
flat. This view was mistaken, those who hold to the correspondence theory will maintain, because the world is *not* flat.
The error lay in people thinking that the claim to flatness
correctly represented the world, when it did not.

The realist will maintain that a statement is *either* true *or*
false. This is to affirm *bivalance*. Bivalence means that a
statement is either true or it is false – whether or not we have
evidence of this truth or falsity. A statement is true if it
successfully corresponds to some reality. Language seeks to

express this reality and sometimes, as in the case of talk of the world being flat, it does so falsely. To talk of truth is to talk of success or of an achievement – it is to claim that language correctly corresponds to the reality that lies beyond it.

On this basis, the statement, "I am sitting on a chair" is true if and only if what I am sitting on is a chair. This seems obvious, but it need not be. In some societies, they may have no idea of chairs – they may never sit down. We could easily imagine a society in which everyone lay down to have meals and the alternatives were between standing and lying down. If someone from such a society were shown a chair she would not know what it was, and might instead regard it as a thing which one stands on in order to make oneself higher – in other words, a form of pedestal. Truth, it might be claimed, is expressed in language and language is used in different ways in different societies. It is this claim that leads onto the alternative conception of truth.

The coherence theory of truth

The coherence theory of truth maintains that a statement is true if it coheres with other true statements. Someone who holds a coherence theory of truth is today called an *anti-realist*.

Imagine a jigsaw. One piece of a jigsaw belongs or is correct only if it fits in with other pieces. Jigsaw pieces are not isolated, they are part of a dynamic whole. All the definitions in a dictionary are in fact circular, since they are all expressed in words, and each of those words is defined by other words. There is no word that cannot be defined using other words.

The coherence theory of truth says that the same sort of principle applies to language. Language is the jigsaw into which words and expressions have to fit. A word that does not fit in does not make any sense. The statement about the world being flat, the anti-realist claims, would once have been

[handwritten top margin: This is what I understand as provisional truth. I draw the conclusion that "Truth is an illusion... Constantly being sought & equally constantly eluding us.]

true because it formed an integral part of the way in which the world was then seen. It was once true, but is so no longer.

According to this theory, as I have said before, a statement is true if it coheres or fits in with other true statements. Take the case of morality. If you are a Roman Catholic, then the statement, "artificial Birth Control is wrong" will be true for you. (You may not, of course, choose to obey this moral rule, but it is nevertheless a rule which forms part of the Catholic way of life.) Similarly, it is true that you have a duty to go to Mass on Sunday and on Holy Days of obligation. If you are a Hindu, it is true that you must respect cows. If you are a Muslim, then it is true that you have an obligation to pray facing towards Mecca and, so far as this is possible, to make a pilgrimage to Mecca at least once during your lifetime.

[handwritten right margin: Here another confu... This statement is NO a ru... AND INDEE IT Assum... That the Catholi way of life is true]

What makes these statements true is that they are part of or fit in with a particular form of life. Within the Catholic, Hindu or Islamic worlds, within their different forms of life, these statements are true. On this basis, there can be different truths in different communities. Truth is not absolute, it is relative. Truth in one culture may be different from truth in another. We can see this very clearly in the case of morality, where different societies have different moral rules and all equally claim that these rules are true. The realist will claim that there is one, absolute morality and that morality within different societies is right or wrong to the extent that it corresponds to this ultimate. The anti-realist claims that there is no absolute morality – moral demands which may be correct in one society are incorrect in another.

Two posts with another post joining them across the top is only a goal post to a society where there is a knowledge of football. What makes this arrangement a goal post is how the society uses the term, and the use it has for the idea of goal posts. In a society which does not play football, the same arrangement might be correctly termed "washing line". In another society it might be called "execution place" – because it is the place from which people are hung by ropes suspended from the cross bar.

The anti-realists hold that truth is relative to the form of life or the community in which it is claimed or expressed. Within a particular form of life, within a particular society, something may be true which is not true elsewhere. Anti-realists deny bivalence (we defined this at the beginning of this chapter), since they claim that some statements are neither true nor false – they just have no content. It is neither true nor false to a tribe of Amazonian Indians who have never seen an outsider before that the three poles form a goal post. The idea of goal posts has simply no meaning for them, and the question of truth or falsity does not, therefore, arise.

* * *

If we consider the moral arena, the issue may be clearer. Take the following statements:

1. Sex before marriage is wrong.
2. Homosexuality is wrong.
3. Killing your parents is wrong.

The realist will maintain that these statements are either true or false and that their truth or falsity does not depend on the society in which they are expressed. Beyond any of our earthly societies, they might perhaps claim, there is a transcendental realm of value which makes moral statements either true or false. If our moral statements correctly correspond to this transcendent morality, then they are true. If they do not correspond, they are false.

The anti-realist will reply, "Oh no, this is not the case at all. Within some societies sex before marriage, homosexuality and killing your parents is wrong, but in other societies these may be right. There are no absolutes. There is no independent standard or vantage point from which or by which we can judge moral norms. Morality evolves to meet the needs of society and in different societies there may be different moralities. A hundred years ago sex before marriage was wrong. Today, in the Western world, it is morally acceptable between two people who love each other and who are in a long-term relationship. In some African societies, sex before marriage is the accepted norm."

If there are disagreements about morality between different societies, the realist will claim that one society is right and the others are wrong, as there can be only one truth. The anti-realist will say that there is no single truth – within each society there are true and valid moral positions, and you cannot judge the morality of one society by the ideas of another.

Someone can be a realist about some things and an anti-realist about others. For instance, someone can be a realist about morality but an anti-realist about the future. Take the statement, "Elizabeth will have sixteen children" made about a girl who is presently aged nineteen and who is biologically capable of having children if the circumstances are right:

1. The realist about the future will maintain that it is either true or false *now* that Elizabeth will have sixteen children, even if we do not know which is the case. Somehow, the realist will maintain, there exists a fact "out there" to which the statement "Elizabeth will have sixteen children" either corresponds or does not correspond. We may not have the evidence to tell whether or not this statement is true, but lack of evidence does not prevent the realist saying that the statement is either true or false.

2. The anti-realist will simply deny that there is any truth to

be known, since there is no fact "out there" and there is no evidence that could count for or against the statement about the number of children that Elizabeth will eventually have.

   The issue of how the realist and the anti-realist make sense of mistakes is important. Both realist and anti-realist recognise that mistakes can be made, but their understanding is different:

1. The realist will seek to justify the truth of a statement by establishing its correspondence with the independent reality to which it is held to relate. A statement will be false if it fails to correspond to the reality that lies beyond language.

    Even when the realist has exhausted *all* the available verification conditions, she will still say, "But I could still be wrong." Truth, for the realist, transcends (or goes beyond) the verification conditions that are or could be available and a *global mistake* is always possible. (A global mistake is a total mistake, a mistake made even after every available or possible checking procedure has been correctly carried out.)

2. The anti-realist will seek to establish the truth of a statement by determining whether it coheres or fits in with other true statements – whether, in other words, it fits in with the jigsaw which is the form of life of the particular society.

    For the anti-realist, a statement is false if it fails to cohere with other true statements within a particular society. The anti-realist checks whether the statement does correctly cohere by applying verification procedures to test the statement against other statements accepted as true within the society concerned.

Once the anti-realist has exhausted all the possible or available checks (the conditions or tests that would verify whether the statement fits into the jigsaw), then the statement is simply held to be true. To continue to say, "Well, we have exhausted the checks – we have used every means to ensure that the statement does cohere with other true statements – but are we *sure* it is true?" simply does not make sense, since truth *is* coherence with other true statements in a particular society or form of life.

A global mistake is, for the anti-realist, impossible. Once we are certain – by applying all the available or possible checking procedures (there is a difference between these two categories which we do not have space to explore here) – that the statement does cohere with other true statements, then the statement in question is simply true.

The difference between realist and anti-realist can be illustrated by the belief in a flat earth which we have used as an example. If we had lived a thousand years ago, all the tests that would have been available would have served to demonstrate that the world was flat. Everyone would have agreed about this, all the best text books would have confirmed it and the evidence would have been overwhelming. The anti-realist would have maintained that in the society in which people were then living it was true to say that the world was flat. The realist, whilst accepting that all the available evidence pointed in this direction, would still have said, "But I could still be wrong." The eventual discovery that the earth was in fact round would, for the realist, have shown that the original claim that the earth was flat was an error, a mistake. It was not correct because the statement did not correspond to the state of the world.

Summary

There are two different ways of looking at what it means to say that a statement is true:

1. The realist claims that a statement is true because it corresponds to a state of affairs that is independent of language and of the society in which we live. To say that a statement is true is to claim that it correctly refers beyond itself.

2. The anti-realist claims that a statement is true because it coheres with other true statements within a particular society or form of life. To say that a statement is true is to claim that it fits in or coheres with other true statements.

When we come to apply this to God, we shall see that the realist maintains that the statement, "God exists" is true because it corresponds or refers to the God who created and sustains the universe. The anti-realist, on the other hand, will claim that "God exists" is true because the statement coheres or fits in with other statements made by religious believers. As we shall see, the two positions are very different!

God is still unlike the Unicorn or the prime number. "GOD EXISTS" is a statement but is meaningless except to God believers.

THREE

The Background to the Debate about God

If you ask someone who speaks Chinese to write down the Chinese symbol for God, he or she may well say, "Which one? The Catholic or the Protestant God?" The Chinese language has a character for each of the two different Gods. Many Christians, of course, would say that this is a mistake and that both Protestants and Catholics worship the same God. This, however, is over-simplistic. There is an enormous difference between the God of traditional Catholic theology and the God with which many Protestants identify – although many Catholics worship the Protestant idea of God and many Protestants think in terms of the Catholic view. In the next four chapters we shall be examining four different conceptions of what it means to talk of God, but before doing this we need to lay some historical foundations.

It has been said by the British philosopher Whitehead that all western philosophy is really a series of footnotes to Plato and Aristotle. We need to start by looking at their two different positions.

Plato

Plato was born in 427 BC and died in 347. He was a native of Athens and came from a noble family. He became a pupil of Socrates. After Socrates was condemned to death for, among other things, "corrupting the young" – by getting them to think for themselves and to challenge the views of their parents and elders – Plato withdrew from Athens and travelled for a number of years. Eventually he returned to his native city and established a school on the outskirts near the grove sacred to Academus. This school, "The Academy", remained in existence until it was dissolved by the Roman Emperor Justinian in 529 AD.

Plato's God was called the Demiurge. The Demiurge did not create matter. Raw matter had always existed in a state of chaos. The Demiurge took this matter and moulded it rather like a potter moulds clay. The potter does not make the clay, but he makes things with it. So the Demiurge used pre-existing matter to fashion the universe. He also enabled the universe to share in his perfection by putting into it mind or soul, which would not otherwise be present in raw matter.

The Demiurge had a model to work from. Plato considered that matter, being in time and space, imperfectly resembled the perfect heavenly Forms which existed outside time and space. Time was "the moving image of eternity" – but it was only an image of the eternal Forms, and could not be identical with them. When people saw, in the universe, examples of truth, justice, beauty or goodness, these were pale reflections of the perfect, timeless and spaceless Forms of Truth, Justice, Beauty and the Good. (Notice that the Forms were written with a capital letter – thus something that was beautiful here on earth imperfectly resembled or participated in the Form of Beauty.) The Forms were not created by the Demiurge and they did not "do" anything. The Forms did not create, nor were they created – they were simply there. The Demiurge used them as a model after which to fashion or make the universe. However, he had a problem.

The Forms were *timeless* (outside time, so that time did not pass for them), *spaceless* (outside space – you could not, therefore, visit one of the Platonic Forms, however far you travelled in a space ship) and *immutable* (unchanging in every respect). The material that the Demiurge had to work with, on the other hand, was temporal and spatial. So the Demiurge had to use imperfect materials to fashion something the original of which was perfect. The universe necessarily, therefore, had to be an imperfect model, because it was in time and space whilst the Forms were not. It is as if a sculptor were asked to make a bronze statue of the wind. Somehow he has to capture in brass the expression of something which is ephemeral, fleeting and changing all the time. He might, for instance, produce a statue of a young girl with her hair being blown free behind her, or one of a tree bending in the wind. The finished sculpture might well capture something of the flavour and power of the wind, but it could not be an altogether accurate picture. Similarly, the Demiurge had to capture in a moving and changing temporal material the essence of something totally unchanging.

The Demiurge did as good a job as he could, but inevitably, given the material he was working with, it was not perfect. This, Plato thought, accounted for many of the imperfections in the world.

The instances of beauty, truth, justice, goodness and similar qualities with which we are familiar on earth are obviously not perfect instances. We know people who are truthful, but that does not mean they are perfectly truthful. We know others who are good, but they are not perfectly good. For Plato, the truthfulness or goodness we see around us is a participation in the perfect Forms of Truth or the Good. These Forms are real and they exist – although in what sense they exist is far from clear.

Everything that we see around us was, for Plato, but a dance of shadows. True reality lay beyond. The finite world is but a pale reflection of the ultimate reality. The fleeting and changing shadows we see around us do not endure. In Plato's view, the philosopher's task must be to free himself from the cave-like world of sense experience in which he is trapped and to look beyond the darkness of the cave which our present world represents to the true reality which can be seen outside it. The body is in a real sense the prison house of the soul. After death my soul, the real me, will, according to Plato, separate from my body and go back to the eternal realm from which it came. Not only will my soul survive death, but it also existed before my birth. When I was born I forgot those things that my soul previously knew. Wordsworth's poem, *Ode to Immortality* expresses this idea clearly: the young boy grows up and forgets the eternal realm from which he came and to which his soul will return. We will explore the different ideas of what it means to talk of a person's soul in a later chapter (p. 193).

It is not at all clear how Plato considered the highest Form, the Form of the Good, to be related to the Demiurge. In the *Timaeus* the Forms are described as the thought of the Demiurge, but since the Demiurge used the Forms as models after which to fashion the universe, he would seem in some sense to be independent of them. Plato did not seem to feel a need to be consistent on this point, but obviously it was a matter that became of concern to later theologians who did not want anything to be independent of their idea of God.

For Plato, therefore, ultimate reality was timeless and spaceless – beyond any sort of change. The Forms were perfect, not because they were moral agents but because they were metaphysically complete and unchanging. They were perfect as they simply existed – the unchanging exemplars or perfect models of those ideas which we see imperfectly represented in our world. It was an attractive idea and was to have an enormous influence in the development of Christian thought.

Aristotle

Aristotle was born in 384 BC and died in 322. In 367 he joined Plato's Academy in Athens. After Plato's death he left Athens and was for a time tutor to the young (thirteen-year-old) boy who later became Alexander the Great. He returned to Athens and, failing to be elected as head of the Academy, founded a rival school called the Lyceum to which he attracted some of the Academy's most distinguished members.

Aristotle rejected many of the ideas put forward by his early master, Plato. In particular he moved away from the idea of the timeless and spaceless Forms. Whereas Plato's thought started from the realm of ideas – with the Forms representing the most truly real of all realities – Aristotle considered that ideas only exist in so far as they are expressed in this world. Thus, rather than the Form of the Good existing in its own right, goodness exists only in so far as people are good.

For Plato, every word had its perfect exemplar. Thus a tree is called a tree because it resembles the perfect Form of "treeness" (Plato appears to have considered that every word we use has its own Form – although there is some debate about this). Aristotle, on the other hand, maintained that the form of something is the unchanging element in it. The form of the tree remains unchanged whilst there can be many and various changes in the appearance of the tree. The form of a thing can be considered as its nature – the form is the reason why something is what it is. As we shall see later (pp. 195ff), Aquinas considered that a human being's soul was the form of his or her body. The form remains the same whilst the human being ages and changes from baby to adult to elderly person. It is the soul as the form of the body which survives death until at some time in the future it is given a new and glorified body.

It was Aristotle who first engaged in the systematic study of logic, and his works on physics and ethics have also had an enormous influence. He maintained that the ideal life for a human being was one of moderation, that nothing should be taken to excess and that virtue always lay between the extremes. As an example, the virtue of courage would lie between the errors of cowardice on the one hand and foolhardiness on the other. "Moderation in all things" might suitably express this approach.

Aristotle can be seen, in a way, as combining God with the Platonic Forms. God, Aristotle considered, was the unmoved mover, the timeless and spaceless creator and sustainer of all, on whom the whole of creation depended. God was the source of all beauty, truth, justice and goodness. This contrasts with Plato, for whom the Forms of Beauty, Truth, Justice and Goodness were apart from the Demiurge who fashioned the universe.

Aristotle defined several different senses of the word "cause". In particular, he considered that everything must have an "efficient cause". The efficient and final cause of the whole universe was God, the unmoved mover.

It was Aristotle who put forward some of the most interesting arguments for the existence of God, and these were to undergo further development at the hands of Christian theologians. For example, since we see things in motion, Aristotle argued, there must be an unmoved mover which set the motion going. Just as the movement of one snooker ball is caused by its being hit by another, and the other's movement is caused by its being hit by yet another. So motion in the world can be explained similarly. However, just as there must be someone to set the first snooker ball rolling, so too, Aristotle considered, there must have been an unmoved mover who set going all motion in the universe. We see causes that operate within the universe – so there must have been a first cause that was not caused by anything else if we are to explain subsequent causes.

In the early years of the Christian Church's development, Aristotle's philosophy was treated with some suspicion and that of Plato tended to be preferred, chiefly because it was thought that Aristotle's ideas inevitably led to a materialistic view of the universe. In addition, the early Fathers were strongly influenced by Plato, so there was a tendency for Aristotle, who was seen to be his main rival, not to be taken seriously. In the sixth century Boethius defended Aristotle's approach, but for hundreds of years after this Aristotle's writings were lost in the West. Eventually they were reintroduced from the East, where they had been preserved by Islamic scholars and had greatly influenced their theology and philosophy. Aristotle was to become the major influence on St Thomas Aquinas and later Catholic philosophy and theology.

It will be readily apparent how attractive the idea of the timelessness and spacelessness of God was to be to later Christian theologians. They wished to hold that God was the creator of all, that the whole of creation depended on him and that he was the source of all life, goodness, justice, truth and beauty. The philosophy of Plato provided the ideal means of expressing these insights and, later, Aristotle's philosophy was used to explain and refine the understanding of religious language.

The biblical approach

On the face of it, the God pictured in both the Old and the New Testaments is very anthropomorphic. Although the highest heaven cannot contain Him, yet God can walk in the garden with Adam, He can wrestle with Jacob and He can blow with his nostrils to part the Red Sea. He can also change his mind – for instance, in Genesis chapter 18 Abraham persuades God not to destroy Sodom for the sake of first fifty, then forty-five, then forty, then thirty, then twenty and finally ten just men in the city. Chapter six says:

> Yahweh saw that the wickedness of man was great on the earth, and that the thoughts in his heart fashioned nothing but wickedness all day long. Yahweh regretted having made man on earth and his heart was grieved. "I will rid the earth's face of man, my own creation," Yahweh said, "and of animals also, reptiles too and the birds of heaven, for I regret having made them."

Here Yahweh regrets having made human beings. It is as if God did not know, when he created them, what they would do. God talks to the prophets and has favourites on no very clear grounds – after all, the "chosen people", Israel, were not selected because they were an especially virtuous, kind or loyal people. The central image, therefore, is of a God who acts and reacts – of a personal God, intimately involved in the fortunes of His people.

As well as this image, however, the Old Testament also emphasises the unknowable character of God. God cannot be seen – no one can see God and live. God's name is never to be spoken and God is above all earthly images. In Islam this strand of Old Testament thinking is still taken very seriously and no picture or statue of God is permitted in any mosque – generally walls are instead decorated with beautifully patterned tiles. Any attempt to capture God's glory or His reality by means of an image would, the Israelites thought, debase him and would be idolatry. They were very clearly aware of the difference between their God and the idols worshipped by the people amongst whom they lived. What is more, God was held to be *omnipresent* – He was present everywhere. The Psalmist puts it this way:

If I ascend to heaven, thou art there! . . .
If I take the wings of the morning
and dwell in the uttermost parts of the sea,
even there thy hand shall lead me
and thy right hand shall hold me.

(Psalm 139:8–10)

And wilt God indeed walk upon the earth?
Behold, Heaven and the highest Heaven cannot contain thee.

(1 Kings 8:27)

In the Old Testament we see God only gradually revealing Himself to His chosen people, and yet He is a God whom they can to some extent understand.

The New Testament continues and accentuates the anthropomorphic image. God is likened to a Father and to a Shepherd; God speaks directly to Jesus; angels come down from heaven and go up again; there is joy in heaven over one sinner who repents; there are mansions in heaven and wine is drunk; someone who has seen Jesus is held to have actually seen the Father. God is, above all, personal and loving. He is an agent who acts in the world.

The picture of God that emerges from the Bible is, therefore, one of a God who can be seen in some ways as a glorified human figure into whose presence we come after death, as if we were coming into the presence of a mighty earthly king. To be sure, the Bible is also aware of the danger of taking this anthropomorphism too far and, particularly in the Old Testament, emphasises the transcendence of God. The Bible never reduces God to a figure like the Greek gods on Mount Olympus or the Norse Gods in Valhalla. The biblical God, unlike Plato's Demiurge, creates the universe *ex nihilo* (from nothing) – God "utters" the world into existence. He says, "Let there be light," and there is light.

The Early Church

The Church Fathers were in a world where the many Roman state gods were either men or else very like human beings indeed. Deceased emperors were deified and some were worshipped as gods while still alive. One reason why the early Christians were so persecuted was that they refused to take part in this worship.

The Church Fathers knew that their God was above all other gods, that he was the source of everything and that the universe depended on him. They knew that God was eternal – but what did this mean? As we shall see, there are two different meanings of the word eternal, and the early Fathers had to choose between them. When they sought to explore ways of understanding God and of talking about Him, the philosophy of Plato was ready to hand and provided the ideal vehicle. So they decided that to talk of God being eternal was to say that He was outside time. The alternative would have been to consider God as everlasting – in other words, within the time series.

A God who was timeless and spaceless, like Plato's Forms, and who was the source of all motion and the cause of all causes, like Aristotle's Unmoved Mover, was clearly far above all lesser gods. No other god could compare with such a reality. If God had been within time, then the problem would have arisen that there would be something (time) outside of God which He had not created. God would not, then, be the creator of everything, since he would be subject to time.

The Church Fathers also wanted God's life to have a quality different to that of our lives – His life could not just be longer than ours. If God were within time, it would be true that He would endure longer than us, but the quality of his life would not be radically different. Timeless existence, however, is a different dimension altogether. The Bible talks of God as being eternal. This is partly to draw a contrast between Him and mere idols which are made and can be broken – they are transient, while the biblical God is far above such limited ideas.

Once one has accepted the idea that the truly perfect, the most ultimately real, must be that which does not change in any way, then the idea of God's timelessness is a logical step. A God outside time could not only create everything in time, but could also be *omniscient* (God could know everything). Timeless God could know the past, the present and the future simultaneously – all times would be present to such a God. This idea has the highly attractive implication that the future is as much present to God as the past, so He knows exactly what the future holds for each of us and His purposes are assured. This means that God's care for us will never be limited by lack of knowledge of what the future might bring. However, this raises the question of whether, if God sees our future, we can really be considered to be free. We shall have to return to this in chapter thirteen.

There may be real advantages in the idea of timeless God, if certain scientific discoveries about the origins of the universe are to be taken seriously. We now know that the universe came into existence with the "Big Bang". Time and space did not exist before the Big Bang – they only started when the universe began. We do not know exactly what happened in the first few thousandths of a second after the Big Bang occurred. Thereafter the course of events is fairly clear. Dense matter exploded apart at enormous velocity, and this matter became the "stuff" and energy out of which the universe was made. Ever since then the universe has been expanding outwards at close to the speed of light in every direction. If time began with the origin of the universe, the idea of a timeless God would seem to make a good deal of sense.

However, advocates of the everlasting God could claim that God's existence pre-dated the Big Bang and that time also existed – measured by reference to the thoughts of this God.

Although the idea of a timeless God is difficult to imagine, St Augustine suggested that it might be approached in this way:

1. Take time and extend it without end in both directions. We then have time that is everlasting – without beginning and without end.

2. Now take this whole time series and roll it into one, so that God has "the complete possession of eternal life all at once" (Augustine) or "the whole, simultaneous and complete possession of eternal life all at once" (Boethius).

All times are simultaneously present to the timeless God. There is no before or after for God, there is no future or past. Instead past, present and future are equally present all at once. Augustine gives us a picture which can help us to imagine this. Think of someone sitting on the top of a mountain and looking down on a road that leads past it. On the road are various people. To those on the road, some people will appear to be in front of them and others will appear to be behind, but to the observer on the mountain all appear simultaneously. So it is with timeless God looking down on the road of time. We are in time, so to us some things are in the past and others are in the future. But to timeless God all times are equally present.

This was an attractive picture and it emphasised the transcendence of God. The view was to be developed by St Thomas Aquinas and remains normative for Roman Catholic theology through to our own time. It does, however, suffer from real problems, and we shall have to examine these in the next chapter.

Summary

There were two main strands of thinking which influenced the early Church Fathers:

1. The Platonic idea that the truly real and truly perfect (The Forms) must be completely unchanging and therefore timeless and spaceless. The Aristotelian modified version of this maintained that the First Cause or Prime Mover was timeless and spaceless.

2. The individual, personal view of God which appeared to be the one put forward in the Bible.

Bringing these two strands together was not easy. The real question was, which strand should be given precedence – which view should be allowed to interpret the other? The two views have been held in uneasy tension throughout the history of Christian thought, and it is a tension which is frequently difficult to resolve. The cover of this book could have borne an illustration of a Rubic's Cube. Understanding God is like understanding the most difficult of all puzzles – a puzzle which we cannot see, which may be beyond time itself and which we can only dimly comprehend. One of the main purposes of this book is to suggest how different ways of understanding God may be fitted together.

In the next chapter we shall see that what it means to talk of God depends to a great extent upon which of the two views above one decides to give priority to.

FOUR

Timeless God – a Realist View

If some ordinary people were discussing black holes, they might well have a vague idea of what they are like. They might know that in a black hole matter collapses in on itself to such a degree that in such a place our whole earth would be reduced to the size of a tennis ball. They might know that the gravitational force of a black hole is so strong that even light itself cannot escape from it, and any object coming near to the hole is sucked into it. However, few people would know much more than this; few people understand just how a black hole works – which is not surprising, as even astrophysicists are unsure.

When we read a book written by a theologian or a philosopher, when we talk to believers and non-believers, when we listen to religious broadcasts on the television or the radio, we will often hear the word God used. It is an integral part of our vocabulary. We are all familiar with it and we all know how to use it. Most of us think we are clear about what it means, but unless we have thought about the matter at considerable length – and sometimes even after we have done this – it is almost certain that our thinking will be mixed up and confused. We know that we are fairly ignorant about black holes, but we feel fairly confident about using the word God. After all, many of us learnt to use the word at our parents' knees, and certainly by the time we arrived at primary school we were familiar with its use.

In fact, understanding what the word God means is a

difficult business – and yet it is tremendously important. Unless we understand what it means to talk of God, we will have great difficulty in making sense of any other religious topic such as prayer, miracles or eternal life. In this chapter we shall be examining four different views of what it means to talk about God. Three of them are realist views, whilst the final one is an anti-realist approach (the differences between these two attitudes have been explored in chapter two).

* * *

In the last chapter we saw that, for the early Church Fathers, it appeared obvious that God must be timeless and spaceless. God, if He were outside space, could not have a body, since bodies were located in space. The Fathers held that God was wholly *simple* (which meant that God could not be divided up into parts – God was God, and did not have arms, legs or any other bodily appendages) and totally *immutable* (God was completely unchanging – God could not be other than God. Since time did not pass for God, God could not change from one state to another).

However, this raised an immediate problem. If God were indeed timeless, spaceless, simple, immutable and omni-scient, God was *very* different indeed from any creature found in the universe. Not only was everything within the universe created whilst God was Creator; not only was every-thing in the universe finite whilst God was infinite; not only was everything in the universe spatial whilst God was outside space, but everything in the universe was in time whilst God was timeless! The differences could hardly have been greater.

Significantly, timeless God is not an individual, so to talk of such a God as He or She is grossly misleading, as gender could only apply to an individual. In fact, we do not have any alternative most of the time – but this is because of the inadequacies of our language. If you look back over the discussion so far, you will see that I have tried to avoid talking of "a timeless God" or even "the timeless God", because "a" and "the" imply that God is in some sense an individual.

How, then, can language which is used to describe created, finite, spatial and temporal things in the universe be applied to God, who is uncreated, infinite, spaceless and timeless? All the words we normally use involve categories that do not apply to God. All the verbs we use – for example, loving, acting, thinking, deliberating, reflecting, knowing or even just existing – involve the concept of time. Since God is so radically different from us, when we use words to talk about Him, those words cannot have the same meanings as they normally have.

Saint Thomas Aquinas is probably fairly described as the greatest theologian that the Christian Church has produced, and his primary concern was this problem – how can the language that the Church uses be applied to God, who is so very, very different from us? His great achievement was to show that the use of such language with reference to God was indeed justified. He was a realist in that he maintained that language about God was true because it corresponded to the reality of God.

Aquinas drew heavily on the philosophy of Aristotle, whose writings had only recently been brought to the Western world by Islamic philosophers who had been studying them for many years, and he combined Aristotelian philosophy with biblical insights. The scholastic approach to philosophy that he founded has dominated Roman Catholic thinking ever since.

Aquinas held that language falls into three categories:

Univocal language

Univocal language occurs where words are used in broadly the same sense in two situations. If, therefore, I say that my wife, Anne, loves me and that my six-year-old daughter loves me, the word "love" is being used in the same way in both cases, even though their love may differ.

Aquinas was adamant that univocal language could not be applied to God, as this would have meant that God was created, finite, temporal and spatial, like human beings. We cannot describe timeless and spaceless God in the same way as we describe temporal and spatial creatures. This, then, is not an available option.

Equivocal language

Equivocal language occurs where the same word is used in two different situations and with totally different meanings. Here are some examples:

1. My cricket bat and the bat in the attic.
2. My fountain pen and the sheep pen in the field.
3. The nut on my bicycle and the nut on the hazel bush.
4. The bar in the gymnasium and the bar in the pub.

In these cases, the same word is being used in two totally different ways. If language about God were equivocal, it would have no content whatsoever for us. I may know what a cricket bat is, but this will tell me nothing whatsoever about what it is to have a bat in the attic.

Analogical language

Analogical language occurs where there is some connection between the way words are used in one sense and the way they are used in another. This language is neither univocal nor equivocal. Take the example which Aquinas himself uses:

1. The bull is healthy.
2. The bull's urine is healthy.

At the time when Aquinas was writing, doctors considered that they could deduce something about the health of an animal or a person by looking at its, his or her urine. If, therefore, they examined a sample of urine and found it to be healthy, they could deduce, since the urine came from the bull, that the bull was healthy. The health of the urine was different from the health of the bull, but the two were nevertheless related, since the latter was the source of the former.

Now let us take another example:

1. God is good.
2. Catherine is good.

We have seen that the word "good", when applied to God, *cannot* mean the same, even on a magnified scale, as it does when applied to Catherine. To say that it can mean the same would be to say that univocal language can be applied to God, and this is not possible. We have no problem in understanding what it means to say that Catherine is good. Catherine is a temporal, spatial creature and our language expresses what it means for her to be good. In addition, we know that there is a connection between Catherine and God. For Aquinas, this connection was established by his "Five Ways" – the five arguments he put forward which he believed showed that it was rational to hold that God existed (we shall look at a derivation of one of these arguments in the next chapter). If God has created all things, then there is a direct connection between God and Catherine, just as there is a direct connection between the bull and its urine.

It is true, therefore, to hold that "God is good", since God must have, as a minimum, whatever is necessary to produce goodness in Catherine. This, Aquinas held, is *analogy of attribution*.

There is, however, another type of analogy – *analogy of proportion*. Aquinas considered that all creatures were created with their own natures. Thus ants, tarantulas, cats, horses, men and angels all have their own distinctive natures, and God's nature is distinctive as well. What it means for an ant to be a good ant, for a cat to be a good cat, for a person to be a good person and for God to be a good God is different in each case.

When we say a person is good, we are saying that he or she is good in whatever way it is appropriate for a person to be good. Similarly, to say that God is good is to say that God is good in whatever way it is appropriate for God to be good.

The great achievement of Aquinas' theory of analogy was to show how language can truthfully be applied to God. But there is a very heavy price to be paid. *We can say that language about God can truly be applied to God, but we do not know what this language means when it is so applied.* The most we can say is that:

1. Under analogy of attribution, God has whatever it takes to create goodness (for instance) in human beings – but we do not know what this is.
2. Under analogy of proportion, it is true that God is good in whatever way it is appropriate for God to be good. We do not, however, know in what way it is appropriate for God to be good.

Aquinas firmly believed that God existed, but he was

42

profoundly agnostic about the nature of God. He held that we can know *that* God is, but not *what* God is. We cannot know God's nature, we cannot know what God is like in Himself. We cannot know what it is for timeless and spaceless God to exist; still less can we know what it is for that God to create, love or suffer. We do know that God is not in time and not in space – we can know certain negative things about God. It cannot be emphasised strongly enough, however, that although it is *true* on this view that God loves, acts, creates and is good, we do not know what these terms mean.

This is a consequence that most people will find very surprising. If you ask a Catholic lay person what it means to say, "God loves me," he will in all probability say that this means that God, who is a spirit, loves him like a father loves his children – only more so. In other words, the assumption will be that univocal language can be applied to God. Catholic theology firmly denies this. It is without doubt true that God loves us, but we do not know what it means for God to love us.

It follows that when reading the Bible one has to interpret the biblical material with this in mind. Talk of God changing his mind is metaphorical – timeless God cannot change his mind, since he cannot be other than he is. Talk of God being angry, knowing or loving does not mean what we mean by these words – God, being timeless, cannot experience emotions. There are no mansions in Heaven – Heaven is timeless, and you cannot have a heavenly society if there is no time. The Bible needs to be interpreted, therefore, by the priest or by the educated person who can understand how its language about God is to be understood in the light of the tradition of the Church. The Church was reluctant to have the Bible translated from Latin into the local languages in the late middle ages because it was feared that untrained people would start to read it and would come to erroneous conclusions.

43

Summary

Those who hold that the timeless, creator God exists are realists. They maintain that the statement "God exists" is true because it corresponds to the existence of a substance which is independent of the universe, which creates it and which can be correctly termed "God". It may be, of course, that they are wrong and that no such substance exists – as philosophical realists they would have to be willing to admit the possibility of error. Their language about timeless God is coherent and what they say about this God fits together, but it is not this coherence that makes the statement "God exists" true.

When we use words about God, these words cannot have the same meaning as when they are used about things or people in the universe. Language about timeless God must be either analogical or metaphorical. The believer can claim that he or she is making true statements about God, without knowing fully what it means for these statements to be true when applied to God.

PHILOSOPHICAL [margin annotation]

I AGREE [margin annotation]

I consider this to be fudging amounting to rubbish. [handwritten annotation]

FIVE

The Everlasting God – a Realist View

The idea of God being timeless and spaceless arose as a result of the priority given to ideas originating in Greek philosophy. They were seen to be intellectually convincing, and so the biblical, personalist picture of God was interpreted in the light of these ideas. This alternative, personalist approach takes the straightforward language of the Bible more seriously and maintains that God is an individual, personal agent. Certainly God is a spirit, but God is an individual spirit with whom the believer can have a two-way relationship. God is perfect in this approach – not in the metaphysical sense that applies to timeless God, whereby He is held to be completely immutable and unchanging – but in a moral sense. God is morally perfect in that his love and care for His creatures and His commitment to them will never change.

The view of God as everlasting is the one that tends to prevail in the Protestant churches. One cannot, however, be firm about this – some Baptists, Methodists and Presbyterians may consider God to be timeless rather than everlasting, and Anglicans may well be fairly evenly divided. Most believers in all churches have never even thought about the issue! Protestants tend to emphasise the individual's personal relationship with God, and the personality of God and of Jesus is at the heart of their beliefs. This does not mean, necessarily, that believers in a timeless God cannot maintain that they have a personal relationship with this God. However, the relationship is difficult to define or envisage, since their God can never change, react, respond or love in the way that these words normally imply.

For the everlasting God, time never began and will never end. At some time, God created the universe out of nothing by his word. At some time in the future, the universe will come to an end, but God will not come to an end. Whether or not there is a universe, God still exists. God has always existed and will always exist. (Notice that this is not something that we can say about timeless God: timeless God did not exist yesterday and will not exist tomorrow – timeless God exists timelessly, and so temporal words simply have no application to this God.)

Einstein has shown us that time is relative. Time slows down as we near the speed of light. This gives rise to the twins paradox. If one twin takes a spaceship at close to the speed of light to the other side of the galaxy and then returns, she may be only ten years older, whilst her twin may have died a hundred years previously. The hymn writer says of God, "A thousand ages in your sight are but an evening gone." So, for God, time may not pass as it does for us – but time still passes! One can imagine being in the presence of God and feeling that hardly any time at all has passed, whilst on earth fifty years may have gone by.

Language about the everlasting God can be univocal. Man is indeed made in the image of God. God can know, be angry, love, remember, change His mind, forgive – and all these words have broadly the same meaning as when applied to human beings. To be sure, God's love is more steadfast and sure than man's love; our love grows cold, and the love of God does not. However, what it means for God to love has much in common with what it means for human beings to love. Biblical language can, therefore, be understood in a univocal way.

This view is highly attractive, but it suffers from three

major problems:

1. The everlasting God can be held to be too anthropo-
    morphic and not sufficiently transcendent. Such a God, it
    may be argued, is rather like a superman. He is too finite
    and not sufficiently different from man.

2. The everlasting God cannot be said to have created time,
    since it has always existed, even before the creation of the
    universe.

3. For timeless God, past, present and future are simultane-
    ously present. The whole of the future is as much present
    to timeless God as is my writing this book, your reading
    it or the extinction of the dinosaurs. To the everlasting
    God, however, the future is future. The everlasting God
    is in time – and to Him, as to us, the future has not yet
    happened. It may therefore be held that the everlasting
    God's omniscience is too restricted.

The first point is not an easy one to answer. Much depends
on what one considers an adequate model of God to be. Some
have held that a timeless God who cannot change and cannot
be other than He is is a lesser reality than a God who is an
infinite, everlasting spirit. There is no easy way of deciding
the issue.

Process theologians, who are influential particularly in the
United States, hold that not only is God in time, but He is also
affected by the universe, and needs it in order to develop and
grow. Through God's interaction with His creation He
changes. God and the world are closely linked, and changes in
the world create real changes in God. Process theology
emphasises God's relationship with His creation and the
centrality of God's love for His creatures. God and the

universe are interdependent. God suffers, loves and develops by interacting with the people He has created. All relationships entail development and, if God can enter into relationships with individuals, it necessarily follows that He changes as the relationship progresses. Instead of the traditional Catholic concept of God as "Being", process theologians emphasise God's "becoming".

Traditionally, Christians have wanted to reject the interdependence of the world and God, since they have held that God created the universe from nothing and still sustains it. The universe without God is nothing, whilst God without the universe is still fully God. Those who accept that God is everlasting could accept this view without going the way of the process theologians, who affirm the interdependence of God and the world. There is no need to take the everlasting model of God as far as the process theologians wish to take it. The extent to which a God who is in time can develop and change is on a kind of sliding scale, and legitimate debate about that scale is possible. Nevertheless, wherever on this sliding scale an individual's view of God is to be located, he or she will still see God as personal and everlasting.

Advocates of the everlasting model of God can reply to the second question raised above by saying that time is not a thing. Before the creation of the universe, with its physical objects which could provide a measure of time, time would still have existed, since God's thoughts would have been sequential. Because God could think, because His thoughts were temporal, time would still have existed. Time has always existed because God has always existed. This in no sense makes time into a "thing" which is external to God.

The third point can be dealt with by saying that God knows everything that it is logically possible to know. God knows the present and perfectly recalls the past. God is *omnipresent* or present everywhere. His presence is not confined to a particular place: "If I take the wings of the morning and flee to the uttermost ends of the earth, you are there . . . " (Psalm 139:9–10). Because of this God can know what is happening in every corner of the universe, and what has happened in their different pasts. God cannot, however, know the future, as the future has not yet happened. There is not yet any future to know. In Chapter Thirteen the whole topic of God's knowledge is dealt with in some detail.

The view that God is an everlasting spirit and that univocal language can be used about Him is probably the most widespread amongst ordinary believers who are not philosophically or theologically trained. They maintain that in prayer an I/Thou relationship with God is possible. Such believers see their relationship with God as being on much the same lines as a relationship between two individuals – although, obviously, God cannot be seen. However, although this is the most common view, we must recognise that truth is not always decided by the ballot box and that ordinary believers are not necessarily the best guide to an understanding of God's nature.

Summary

Those who maintain that God exists everlastingly are realists. They maintain that the statement, "God exists" is true because it corresponds to the existence of an incorporeal spirit who can correctly be referred to by the word "God". As philosophic realists, they would have to admit that they could be wrong and that no such God exists. Their talk about this God is coherent and fits together, but it is not this coherence that makes the statement "God exists" true.

The chief problems connected with the idea of an everlasting God are that such a God may look too much like a cosmic superman, and that, being in time, He may not be able to know the future. However, believers can apply language to this God in much the same way as they apply it to things in the world – in Thomist terms, univocal language can be used about God.

SIX

Talk of God as Talk about an Alternative Lifestyle – a Realist View

1. In the second chapter we defined realism.

2. A revisionary view of Christianity is, for the purposes of this book, defined as one that retains much of the language of Christianity but dispenses with the idea of a creator God who sustains and interacts with the universe.

The view put forward here combines these two approaches.

In the desert, the New Testament says, Jesus was tempted by the Devil. He offered Jesus glittering prizes if he would only worship him. Jesus resisted all three temptations, and then the Devil left him. Few theologians today, however, think that there is a personal Devil. The medieval idea of a Devil with horns and a thrashing tail is a thing of the past. This does not, however, invalidate the story of the temptations. Jesus was, indeed, subject to temptation. In the wilderness he clearly wrestled with real choices about how his life was to be lived. He could have chosen to seek power, or to cater for people's material needs. Instead he sought an alternative way.

If, then, we can make sense of the temptations in the wilderness without postulating a personal Devil, why can we not similarly make sense of Jesus' prayer in the Garden of Gethsemene without thinking in terms of a personal God? Once again, Jesus was wrestling with real alternatives. He knew what was likely to happen. He knew that his death was highly probable. He could have escaped, he could have compromised with the Temple authorities – but he refused to do so. Jesus was struggling with real choices, and we do not need to believe that there was a God-figure listening to him in order to be able to make sense of this temptation.

It is in these terms that Professor Stewart Sutherland puts forward his revisionary account of Christian belief (in *God, Jesus and Belief*, Blackwell, 1984). Sutherland considers that there is much which is of value in Christianity, and that it is important that it should be preserved and retained. However, if Christianity is to be credible for the next century, it can no longer think in terms of a personal God. In particular, Sutherland rejects any appeal to revelation – how, after all, does one choose the revelation to which one will listen? Also, Sutherland starts from the facts about the world, and we know that the world includes much suffering and evil. Because of these considerations, he maintains that we cannot retain a belief in the God of traditional theism, a God both all-powerful and all-good. In the past believers have started with an assumption about God and his attributes and have then tried to resolve the problem of evil that necessarily arises. Sutherland does not think that this can be done, and he maintains that all attempts to resolve the problem of evil fail. However, he thinks there is real value in the insights of Christianity and proposes a revisionary view which makes and defends a claim to truth and preserves the essential Christian message.

Having rejected the traditional idea of a God who created the universe and who is apart from it (in other words both the timeless and everlasting models of God are rejected), Sutherland sets out an alternative way of understanding religious language. He openly admits that he is a revisionist – he is trying to revise the essential Christian ideas so that Christianity's insights about how human beings can live their lives can be maintained into the next century. Talk of an everlasting or timeless God is no longer credible, so an alternative way of understanding religious language is needed.

In Robert Bolt's play *A Man For All Seasons*, Thomas More, the Lord Chancellor of England, tells the young and ambitious courtier named Rich, who has come to him seeking advancement, that he is on the wrong path in life. More says: "Go and be a teacher. If you are a good teacher, you will know it, your pupils will know it and God will know it." According to Sutherland's revised Christianity, "and God will know it" does not mean that there is a CIA (Celestial Intelligence Agency) in the sky which will monitor Rich's every action. Instead it means that there is a way in which the young man can live his life which cannot be trivialised. There is a way of living life that is not vulnerable to the way things turn out. So many of our objectives in life – whether these be money, power, reputation or success – are trivialised and rendered meaningless by events outside our control. If, however, we seek to live a good life – a life lived for others, a life of compassion and love – then nothing can take this away from us.

Socrates said that nothing could harm the good man. Certainly Socrates knew that the good person could be hurt – he or she could be tortured and could lose his or her possessions. However, at the end of the day nothing can take away from such an individual the commitment he or she has made to a life lived for others. Even death itself cannot trivialise a life of compassion and saintliness. The holy person has eternal life – not in the sense of life after death but in the sense of a different quality of life in this world. There is no outward form of the holy life. The essential characteristic of holiness is an inner orientation.

Christianity is an optimistic religion, Sutherland argues, as it maintains that the life of holiness is a real possibility. The person who is kind, loving and unselfish, the person who puts others into first place, is not mad or deluded. Jesus was the person who showed us that such a life could be lived. He was the perfect example – he showed that it could be done. What had before been a mere possibility (just as unicorns and man-eating flies are mere possibilities which we can imagine but which do not actually exist), with Jesus became a *real possibility*. Before the Americans landed a man on the moon, this was a mere possibility. It was possible in theory, but it had never been done. When Neil Armstrong walked on the moon, the mere possibility became an actuality.

Jesus showed that a life of self-giving love and saintliness could be lived. He did it, he lived it. He showed that what had previously been a merely possible way of living life could be actualised. Christianity calls people to the life of holiness. Because Jesus lived it, it is a real possibility.

Now this sounds very odd. How can one be a realist about possibilities? The answer lies in the difference between "mere possibilities" and "real possibilities". Many things are merely possible – Jesus, by living his life, showed that the life of holiness is really, actually possible. It is a genuine option. Talk about God is talk about the life of sanctity. Talk about God is true, theology is true, because it is talk about a way of life that is a real possibility. That is why this section is headed, "Talk of God as talk about an alternative lifestyle".

Sutherland makes a major claim about his view which shows his affinity to Plato. He says he is making *an ontological commitment about the nature of reality*. This sounds complicated, but is not as bad as it sounds! What it means is that Sutherland is claiming that reality, the universe itself, is such that someone can live the life of holiness and not be deluded. The commitment is an ontological one because Christianity claims that it is telling us something about the very nature of reality.

The word "ontology" means that we are discussing the nature of being, or the nature of reality. Reality is such that even if all human beings died out, a future race of intelligent green toads could discover the possibility of the holy life that would be available, waiting to be lived out.

The reference to intelligent green toads (although my example and not Sutherland's) is significant. It shows that the life of holiness is not something relative to human beings. The very fabric of the universe is such that it can tolerate the life of self-giving love. Any intelligent race could, therefore, discover this reality which is waiting to be found. Questions could be asked about *why* the universe is such that it is possible for a good life to be lived, and on the basis of this fact a form of design argument for the existence of God might be constructed. Sutherland himself, however, does not attempt to formulate such an argument.

Christianity, then, calls people to a different way of living. It calls people to eternal life – to a life lived, as Sutherland puts it, "*sub specie aeternitatis*". "Eternal" here does not refer to any eternal realm. It rather refers to a different way of viewing life. Instead of seeking material ends, we should seek spiritual ends. Sutherland is at best agnostic about the existence of any God or life after death, and considers that they would be irrelevant even if they did exist. The important matter is how we live our lives now – it is with this that Christianity should be primarily concerned. New Testament passages such as the following could be quoted to support this approach: "This is eternal life, that they know thee, the only true God, and Jesus Christ whom thou has sent" (John 17:3); "Truly, truly I say unto you, he who hears my word and believes him who sent me, has eternal life" (5:24). These emphasise eternal life as a different quality of life here and now, not as something that occurs after death.

Critics might say, "But Sutherland is just reducing Christianity to a form of morality. In his view, we no longer need religious language. We can do away with talk about God and theological language in general, and instead substitute language about morality. Why talk about God? Instead we can talk about living a kind and good life." However, Sutherland specifically claims that there is more to religious language than this, and rejects the charge that he is a reductionist.

In Sutherland's view, religious language calls us beyond our present moral certainties. It can never call us to act against morality, but it may show us that certain actions which we have previously thought of as acceptable are, in fact, not so. Jesus gave an example of such a religious demand when he said that his followers should not simply refrain from committing adultery, but should not even think about it! Similarly, Wilberforce rejected the morality of his time, which accepted slavery, and appealed to a religious way of life (a view of life *sub specie aeternitatis*) to show that society's existing morality was inadequate and must be changed. The same can happen today – religion can (or should!) challenge our accepted views on, for example, racism, sexism or the affluence of the western world. Religious language, therefore, calls people out beyond the frontiers of their existing morality to a different way of living life – but it can never call people to act immorally.

Some, of course, would reject the possibility of living a saintly life altogether, seeing no point in it. They would say that anyone seeking to live a life of self-giving love was crazy – that Mother Teresa should instead seek pleasure and enjoyment for herself; that Archbishop Tutu should spend more time on holiday with his family and less worrying about political structures which do not affect him personally very much. Sutherland is saying not just that this is a possible point of view, but that such a point of view is *wrong*. He is a realist, but a realist of a special kind. He is a realist, as we have seen, about possibilities.

The word "God", therefore, does not refer to some being who created and sustains the world. To use theological language – for instance, to talk of "God's will" or "God's power" or to say, "God will know it" – is not to refer to a being who has a will or who is powerful or who knows things. Instead, such language calls us to look at our lives in a different way; to live for others and to die to our selfish interests.

This view has many attractions. Although Sutherland is proposing a revisionist account of Christianity, his approach could be extended to other religions as well. Talk of Allah, Jehovah or Nirvana can be seen as affirming the possibility of a different way of looking at and living life. Religious language challenges the normally accepted priorities of the world of materialism and shows that an individual can live in an entirely different way. It is a way that the world may regard as foolish and that may bring no apparent return except for persecution, opposition and suffering, and yet it is, at the same time, ultimately fulfilling and worthwhile. In a world in which there is great religious diversity, all the major world religions can be seen as calling their people to live life *sub specie aeternitatis* – to live "in the eternal" in this world, rather than to hope to survive death.

We must also recognise that there are difficulties with this revision of Christianity. Sutherland calls us to a noble and virtuous life, but living it is going to be a lonely business. There is no possibility of living out a relationship of love with the God who created us, so that His love shows forth in the way we treat other people. Perhaps this is not necessary, but many Christian saints might say that it was only this relationship which sustained and made possible the lives they lived. Also Sutherland takes no account of the claimed resurrection of Jesus as an individual on Easter Sunday, nor of the hope of personal life after death which Christianity has always affirmed. To be sure, this hope cannot be proved, but the experiences of people who have been very close to death often do seem to point to something beyond the grave – although such evidence is far from conclusive. Finally, Sutherland is not clear on exactly how we would determine what the life *sub specie aeternitatis* calls us to. It seems a very individualistic vision, and interpretations of it may well differ markedly.

Having said this, however, Sutherland's approach has great strengths, and it is particularly distinctive in that it is the only revisionist view of Christianity currently available which still maintains a realist position about truth.

Summary

Talk about God, in Sutherland's view, is talk about a different way in which life can be lived. There is no God and no life after death. This is a realist view, since it claims that the truth of Christian language depends on the universe being such that it makes sense to live a life of holiness. The claim of Christianity to be true is a claim that it is possible that a person can live a life of self-giving love and not be mad or otherwise deluded. Christianity could, of course, be wrong – this a realist will always be willing to admit – and in this case the life of sanctity is simply foolishness.

The crucial point about Christianity is how its followers live out the Christian message. Whether or not God exists and whether or not we, as individuals, survive death is simply irrelevant.

This attacks me. Drop God and it is Humanism

SEVEN

God as a Reality within a Religious Form of Life – an Anti-realist View

SECOND

1. In the first chapter we defined anti-realism.

2. A revisionary view of Christianity, for the purposes of this book, is one that retains much of the language of Christianity but dispenses with the idea of a creator God who sustains and interacts with the universe.

It will be obvious from the above definitions that both the view put forward in this chapter and the view covered in the previous one are revisionary – the difference between them lies in the fact that whereas Sutherland's view is realist, the ideas put forward in this section are anti-realist. As we shall see, the difference is highly significant.

Wittgenstein is probably the most influential philosopher of the twentieth century, even though there are many different opinions about what exactly he was saying. His work can broadly be split into two periods – that of the early Wittgenstein, who wrote the *Tractatus*, and that of the later Wittgenstein, who wrote *On Certainty* and *Philosophic Investigations*. The latter is not an easy book to read, as it is a series of points whose connections are not always obvious. Wittgenstein wanted to make his reader work at understanding him, and whilst this is a laudable aim, it does mean that opinions can differ as to the meaning of his writings.

In his later work, Wittgenstein was concerned with how

language is used. Language, he maintained, is a public affair – the idea of a private language does not make sense. Language is also dynamic, and words can have many meanings. The same word or phrase can mean different things in different situations. Nowhere is this more true than in the area of religious language.

A. J. Ayer and the logical positivists had maintained a *verification theory* of meaning. They held that a statement was meaningless unless the conditions which could *verify* it (i.e. which could show it to be true) could be stipulated. Out of this, Anthony Flew developed the *falsification theory* which demanded that, if any sentence were to be meaningful, the conditions which could *falsify* it (i.e. which could show it to be false) had to be stated. Both the verificationists and the falsificationists wished to dismiss religious language as having no meaning, since it could be neither verified nor falsified (how, after all, would one verify the claim, "God loves me"?) These theories broke down because their advocates had to admit so many possible exceptions to their general rules. John Hick also replied to them with his idea of *eschatological verification* – the claim that religious statements would be verified after death. In other words, Hick claimed that statements such as "God loves me" or "Jesus is the Son of God" could be verified as being true by the believer who survived death.

Wittgenstein saw the inadequacy of the logical positivist's approach and, in contrast to his early days, when he wrote the *Tractatus*, now had a more modest view of philosophy. He regarded philosophy as being a second-order activity which must leave everything as it is. The objective of philosophy was to understand, not to lay down what could and could not be said (which is what the verificationists and falsificationists wished to do).

Rene Descartes and John Locke both believed that human

knowledge had to have foundations. Descartes believed that these foundations were internal, that they were ideas in the mind. Locke believed that the foundations for knowledge were sense experiences. He was an *empiricist* – he believed that the final arbiters of certainty were those things which could be experienced. Saint Thomas, one of Jesus' apostles, was also an empiricist when he said, "Unless I see in his hands the print of the nails, and place my finger in his side, I will not believe" (John 20:25). Wittgenstein rejected the whole idea that knowledge has foundations.

We are each educated into a particular form of life. We grow up into a certain way of looking at the world. This form of life, this way of looking at the world, is given expression in our language. Language expresses a form of life. When we claim to know something, this is a claim to an achievement, and it requires justification. In order to show that I know how to fly an aeroplane, I would have to demonstrate that I could fly – for instance, by producing my pilot's licence or by getting into an aeroplane and flying it. However, the most basic claims made by language are not justified – they are groundless. This needs some explanation.

In *On Certainty* Wittgenstein discussed G. E. Moore's famous paper, *In Defence of Common Sense*. Wittgenstein showed that language makes contact with the world by certain banal, obvious statements which are groundless. These statements are not justified and do not require justification – there are no grounds for holding them. Statements like, "This is a hand", "There is a bookcase" and "This is a chair" are learnt at our parents' knees and *it simply does not make sense to doubt them*. We cannot justify the claim that "This is a hand" – in the sense it is a groundless belief, a belief held without grounds to support it. We were simply educated into calling certain things hands, bookcases and chairs. If anyone in our society seriously doubts that what I am sitting on is a chair, then there is something wrong with him or her!

As Norman Malcolm says, it is hard to appreciate the extent to which our most basic beliefs are groundless – and nowhere is this more so than in the case of religion. The believer believes in God – he does not doubt this. Belief in God is, rather, the precondition for all doubting and questioning. Just as we learn about tables and chairs at our mother's knee, and these basic propositions are groundless, so belief in God, advocates of this view hold, does not rest on evidence or grounds.

The way language is used in one form of life cannot judge the way it is used in another. Scientific language cannot, for instance, judge religious language. Wittgenstein (writing during the Second World War) asks us to imagine one person saying to another:

1. "I believe there is a German aeroplane overhead." The reply is:
2. "Well, possibly."

Then we are asked to contrast this with:

1. "I believe there is a Last Judgement."
2. "Well, possibly."

While "Well, possibly" is a sensible reply to the first belief claim, which is tentative in nature, it is not an appropriate reply to the second belief claim. Belief in the Last Judgement is a belief of a different order and magnitude to that of the first belief. It is not a tentative belief but rather a belief which shapes the whole of the way a believer looks at the world.

Take another example. Imagine a believer saying: "I am in pain. This is a punishment for sin. Don't you agree?" Wittgenstein says that he would be unable to answer either "Yes" or "No". When he thinks of pain, he does not think of sin. His mind does not work like that – he does not use ideas like sin to make sense of his world.

One form of life may, therefore, not be able to understand another, and it certainly cannot judge another by its own terms. The non-believing scientist may hear the Catholic believer saying, "This is the blood of Christ." If the scientist then grabs the consecrated wine, rushes to her laboratory and carries out an analysis for the presence of blood, she has failed to understand how religious language works. It is more complicated than that. As Wittgenstein put it: "For a blunder, that's too big."

Time and again, when one society meets another, it will judge the other on its own terms. The westerner meeting the Indian tribe which decides whether a man and a woman should get married by looking at the entrails of a chicken, or which carries out rain dances every year, is likely to dismiss these practices as superstitious and nonsensical. Similarly, the scientist will dismiss the Catholic's claims – and in so doing almost certainly misunderstands them. The more we study tribal societies, the more depth and profundity do we find there. If we would understand their way of life or the way of life of Catholic believers, we must study their forms of life as entireties. We must see what role is performed by talk of rain dances or of the blood of Christ. We must seek to understand how their languages express their forms of life.

It is rather like someone watching a game when they do not know the rules. If an Englishman watches a game of American football, it may at first seem incomprehensible, but after a time he may come to appreciate the rules according to which the game is played. So the non-believer should seek to understand how believers use language, how their language expresses their form of life. The term "language" covers not just the words used but also the beliefs, practices and rules associated with a form of life. Wittgenstein talked of language games, but the word "games" can be misleading and can wrongly trivialise the point Wittgenstein wished to make. He was saying that if we are outsiders to a form of life and to the language with which this form of life is expressed, we must seek to understand the rules by which the language works. One form of life cannot judge another on its own terms.

Wittgenstein's contemporary disciples use his ideas (although I personally think it is arguable whether or not they accurately reflect his own views!), and their thinking is growing in significance and importance. In terms of sheer volume and scope of writing, the books by Dewi Phillips are notable. They are influential and generally easy to read. Don Cupitt is certainly the best known revisionist of traditional Christianity. His books are also easy to read and his arguments are attractive. However, he is not as directly influenced by Wittgenstein as Phillips is, and so I have not dealt with his approach here. However, to those who find anti-realism attractive, Don Cupitt's books are worthwhile reading. A list of some of Phillips' and Cupitt's writings is given at the end of this book. A lesser-known figure is a Dominican priest, Fr. Gareth Moore, whose book *Believing in God* (T. & T. Clarke, 1988) sets out what he considers Christianity to involve when Wittgenstein's approach is taken seriously.

Moore's book ends with the key statement, "People do not discover religious truths, they make them." This expresses his position clearly. A realist would say the opposite. A realist claims that people do not make religious truths, they discover them. The truth of a realist claim is based on its correspondence to reality – the truth of an anti-realist claim is based on coherence. "God exists" is true, not because the word "God" refers to an everlasting being or a timeless substance, but rather because the phrase, "God exists" has a use and a purpose within the form of life of the believing community.

If we look at a Christian community (or indeed a Muslim, Hindu, Sikh or Jewish community), then the language that this community uses to talk about its religious beliefs clearly has a value. Religious language gives expression to the religious form of life. The Christian believer considers that God exists; that God is love; that God helps the believer; that Jesus is remembered at or is present in the bread/body and wine/blood of Christ taken at the Eucharist (depending on whether one is a Baptist, Methodist, Presbyterian or Reformed church member on the one hand or a Catholic on the other – Anglicans tend to be divided between the two positions).

The outsider to religion must seek to understand how this language is used. We have already said that rushing off to the laboratory and analysing the eucharistic wine is a basic mistake, so to understand religious language we must see the role it plays in the lives of believers. "God is nothing," Gareth Moore continually says. God is not some individual, some object or some being like Charlie. Aquinas maintains that God is "no thing": God is timeless substance and is not an individual. However, Moore goes much further than that – his approach is to maintain that God really is nothing. God does, however, exist as a reality within the form of life of the believing community.

For the believer, God exists, but God does not exist for the non-believer. This is not a dispute about a matter of fact in which one is right and the other is wrong. Rather, it is a dispute about whether terms like "God", "prayer" or "Last Judgement" have a role in the believer's life.

When one converts from non-belief to belief, one enters a new form of life and one has to learn how the language of this form of life is used. The priest is (says Moore) the "grammatical expert" who knows how the language of the Church is to be employed. The convert has to undergo instruction or initiation into the new language. The Catholic Rite for the

Initiation of Adults might involve, on this view of things, communicating to the convert the truths of the Catholic language game – teaching him the grammatical rules of the Catholic form of life. Within this form of life, some things can be said and others cannot. Catholics are required to assent to certain beliefs – for instance, belief in the assumption of the Virgin Mary and in Papal Infallibility. These claims are true because they cohere or fit in with other Catholic truths, and someone who cannot assent to them cannot be a Catholic.

It cannot be emphasised strongly enough that, in this way of thinking, God exists. God really, really, truly, truly exists. But God does not exist as a creator who is distinct from the world; He is not some being who is apart from the world and who sustains it and acts in it. God is instead a reality within the believing community.

[margin note: FOR THOSE SO INDOC- RINAT]

Prime numbers provide us with a helpful parallel. To the non-mathematician, prime numbers are not real; they do not exist. The mathematician, however, is in no doubt at all about their existence. If someone learns mathematics, he or she comes to learn about prime numbers; he or she learns about how the language of prime numbers is used. For such an individual, prime numbers become a reality, while previously they were not. Once the individual has seen the reality of prime numbers, nothing can make them unreal to him or her. Mimicking the Psalmist's words, the person might say: "If I take the wings of the morning and flee to the uttermost ends of the earth, even there prime numbers will be with me," or perhaps, "Nothing can separate me from the reality of prime numbers."

Prime numbers certainly exist – but not in the same way as chairs. God, in this view of things, certainly exists – but not in the same way as any being or individual. God is an existing reality, found within the form of life of the believing community, where language about God has meaning and value.

Language about God is true, since it coheres or fits in with the other language used by the religious believer.

The importance of community is vital to this view. Revisionary realism is an individual approach to Christianity and could well, therefore, appeal to Protestants – it holds that Christianity involves the individual seeking to live life *sub specie aeternitatis*. Revisionary anti-realism is much more community-orientated because it maintains that the reality of God is found and expressed in language – and is not independent of language. Since the Second Vatican Council the Catholic Church has heavily emphasised the idea of community. Increasingly, being a Catholic is seen to be to belong to the Catholic community. Community is central. The same is true of the anti-realist approach. It is within the community that God's reality is found, and it is the language of the community that gives this reality expression.

In some ways this view can be seen as a development beyond the idea of a timeless God. It is the result of the progressive process of abstraction that has taken place in mankind's thinking about God. God can no longer, in this view, be thought of as a spiritual being or a timeless substance. Instead the existent reality that is God is found within the believing community. As Jesus said: "Wherever two or three are gathered together in my name, I will be with them." The believer, once he or she has come to understand what the term "God" means, can never be separated from this reality.

Rationally, this approach has many strengths. It does, however, suffer from significant weaknesses as well. It does not take seriously claims of mystical and religious experiences of a loving creator God. It is also prescriptive in that it lays down what it is that believers are doing. This approach is said to stem from Wittgenstein, and yet it flies in the face of his demand that philosophy should "leave everything as it is". Christian believers almost universally *do* believe in a creator

God who interacts with the universe, and they use this language in a realist sense – even if they are not aware that they are doing so!

In the chapters that follow we shall be exploring the meaning which this approach gives to talk about prayer, miracles, eternal life and other religious terms. Clearly, as God is not an agent outside the universe, there will need to be some revision of the way in which religious language is understood – but this is, after all, a revisionary view!

Summary

God, in this view, really exists. The statement "God exists" and the religious language that goes with it are true. However, truth is based on coherence within a particular community or form of life. The word "God" does not refer to some everlasting spirit or timeless substance; God is not an individual. Different truths are being affirmed by different forms of life.

One form of life cannot judge another – the language of science cannot judge that of religion nor can religion judge science. Hindu truths, Muslim truths and Christian truths are all true – but there is no single absolute truth. Truth is relative. The believer, when he or she converts from non-belief, comes to find a use for language about God, where previously that language had no place in his or her life. In finding the value of religious language, the individual finds God. Believers do not discover religious truths – they make them.

SURELY THE VALUE IS MERELY THE FACT
THAT COMMUNICATION CAN TAKE PLACE
IN THIS CLUB.

EIGHT

The Cosmological Argument

It should by now be obvious that the word God has many meanings. Those who believe in a timeless or everlasting God maintain that statements about Him are true because they correspond to the reality of God, who exists independently of anything in the world. Obviously, it will be important for them to show that the creator God exists – after all, many people deny that there is such a God.

If we want to prove that something exists, we first need to know what it is. If I were to ask you to find an aardvark, you might reasonably first want to know what an aardvark is – if you did not, it might be exceedingly hard to find one! In many ways, therefore, the sensible starting point when looking at arguments for God's existence would be to consider each of the different views of God that we have so far considered.

In fact we are not going to work this way round. The reason is that the arguments for the existence of God are well defined and well known in philosophic circles. So we shall start by looking at the arguments, in the case of each considering the view of God to which it points. It is important to recognise that different arguments point to different conceptions of God.

First we shall look at the Cosmological Argument and then, in succeeding chapters, we shall move on to the Ontological Argument, the Design Argument and finally the Argument from Religious Experience.

* * *

The term "cosmological" derives from the word "cosmos", meaning "the universe". The Cosmological Argument is an argument that starts from the existence of the universe and tries to prove from this that God exists. The argument depends on a willingness to ask the question, "Why is there a universe?" After all, the universe exists and it might not have done. If we are not interested in the question, if we just say, "Well, the universe is just there and that's all there is to it." Then the argument will not get off the ground.

The Cosmological Argument has one tremendous advantage. It starts from an invulnerable first premise which we all accept – the existence of the universe. It is *an a posteriori argument* – an argument which starts from something we experience, in this case the universe. The steps in the Cosmological Argument may be challenged, but its starting point is undoubted.

Leibniz, in his *Theodicy* (written in 1710) put the Cosmological Argument forward as follows:

> Suppose the book of the elements of geometry to have been eternal, one copy having been written down from an earlier one. It is evident that even though a reason can be given for the present book out of a past one, we should never come to a full reason. What is true of the books is also true of the states of the world. If you suppose the world eternal, you will suppose nothing but a succession of states and will not find in any of them a sufficient reason.

Leibniz says that "the great principle" of the Cosmological Argument is that "nothing takes place without a sufficient reason." This is known as *the Principle of Sufficient Reason*. By a "sufficient reason" Leibniz means a complete explanation. Thus, to explain the existence of one book by saying that it is copied from another or to explain your existence by saying that you were a child of your parents only gives a partial explanation. If there is going to be a complete or sufficient reason for the book or for your existence, we have to get back to something which does not depend on anything else – and this will be God.

Leibniz is saying that if we suppose the world to be everlasting – to go on and on, backwards in time for ever – we will never come to a complete or sufficient explanation for its existence. We should not be satisfied with such an unending regress, he claims, but should instead recognise that the whole universe depends on God, who is uncaused and does not depend on anything else.

The question is, of course, whether we have to accept the Principle of Sufficient Reason. Is it any more improbable that each state of the universe should be explainable by a previous state – going on and on to infinity – than that the universe should depend on an uncaused God? Scientists do now know that if we go back in time to the very beginnings of the universe, time ceases to exist at the moment of the "Big Bang". The universe and time itself started with the Big Bang. This, perhaps, may make it less plausible to claim that each state of the universe can be explained by a preceding state. If, as critics of the Cosmological Argument claim, God was not the cause of the Big Bang, they need to suggest what the cause was.

The Cosmological Argument has been reformulated and put into a more modern form by the leading Jesuit Philosopher, Professor F. Copleston. He put his version forward in a debate with Bertrand Russell on BBC Radio in 1947. His argument is shorter than that constructed by St Thomas Aquinas in the third of his "Five Ways" of providing the existence of God, although the reasoning is very similar to that of Aquinas whilst avoiding some unnecessary steps. Copleston's version can be summarised as follows:

1. We know that there are some things in the world which
    do not contain within themselves the reason for their own
    existence.

In other words, there are things in the universe which are
contingent or not self-explanatory. They are "might-not-
have-beens" because, like you and I, they might not have
existed (if, for instance, our parents had not met).

2. The world is simply the real or imagined totality of
    individual objects, none of which contain within them-
    selves the reason for their own existence.

Copleston is saying here that everything within the universe is not self-explanatory. He moves from 1. above, in
which he claims that some things depend on others, to saying
here that all things in the universe depend on other things. All
things within the universe can only be explained by some
cause or reason external to them.

3. Therefore the explanation for the existence of everything
    in the universe must be external to the universe.

Once we have accepted the second premise, then, *if* we
accept Leibniz's Principle of Sufficient Reason – his insistence
that there must be a full and complete explanation – it follows
that outside the universe there must be a cause for everything
in the universe.

4. This explanation must be an existent being which is
    self-explanatory – in other words, a being which contains
    within itself the reason for its own existence. This Cop-
    leston refers to as a necessary being.

If everything within the universe is contingent or dependent, then, if we have accepted 3., the final explanation must be
necessary – in other words, this final explanation could not

not exist. It could not fail to exist; it is not dependent on anything else. This final explanation Copleston considers to be God.

Copleston defined a necessary being as "a being that must and cannot-not exist". Bertrand Russell responded to Copleston largely by rejecting his terminology. Once you accept the terminology, particularly the claim that everything in the world is either contingent or dependent, then the argument becomes much more persuasive. Once one accepts that everything is dependent upon something else, then it follows that something must be necessary or non-dependent. Russell avoided this by refusing to accept the use of the term "contingent" or the notion of dependence. He said in reply to Copleston: "I should say that the universe is just there, and that is all."

Copleston's response to this is significant. He said:

If one does not wish to embark on the path which leads to the affirmation of transcendent being, however the latter may be described, one has to deny the reality of the problem and assert that things "just are" and that the existential problem in question is just a pseudo-problem. And if one refuses to even sit down at the chess board and make a move, one cannot, of course, be checkmated.

As I said at the beginning of this chapter, the Cosmological Argument depends upon a willingness to ask the question, "Why is the universe here?" If one is willing to accept that the universe is just a brute fact, then the question does not get posed and the answer, "God", will not be required.

David Hume argued that it was illegitimate to move from saying that every event in the universe has a cause to the claim that therefore the universe has a cause. Bertrand Russell made a parallel point by remarking that this was rather like moving from saying that every human being has a mother to the claim that the human race as a whole has a mother. It is quite correct to claim that all humans have mothers (or at least that they come from a female egg cell – the advance of fertilisation and embryo research may soon mean that it will not be necessary for a woman to actually carry a baby in her womb, and instead it could be developed in an incubator for the full nine months), but it is certainly not correct to claim that the human race as a whole has a mother. One cannot move from individual causes to a claim that the totality of all has a cause.

Copleston considers we should ask for an explanation of the universe, while Russell maintains that we should not. If we were to push Russell by saying, "But everything requires an explanation, and so the universe must therefore require an explanation," and if Russell were then to agree with us (which, given his argument in the previous paragraph, would be unlikely), we might then arrive at God as the explanation for the universe's existence. However, Russell would then be able to turn the tables on us by saying, "If everything requires an explanation, what is the explanation for God?" We could not easily refuse to explain God when we had denied Russell the right to refuse to explain the universe. Why should God be self-explanatory in a way that the universe itself is not? It is this problem that supporters of the Cosmological Argument need to overcome.

Martin Lee rejects the Cosmological Argument ("Why is there something rather than nothing?", *Heythrop Journal*, 1985) because, he maintains, God must be either something or nothing. If God is something, then we can ask for reasons why this something exists, and so the ultimate "Why" question would not be solved by positing the existence of God. If God is nothing, then God could not be an agent who created the universe. Lee accuses Aquinas of trying to say that

God is neither something nor nothing – rather, a special category somewhere between the two. This, Lee maintains, is not a possible position. Lee's challenge is a good one, but it does not necessarily disprove Aquinas' case. Lee uses the terms "something" and "nothing" univocally and, as we have seen, Aquinas rejects such use of language. Aquinas would be quite happy to say that God transcends the distinction between something and nothing – and this is exactly what he, Aquinas, is saying. Whether or not this is valid is an open question.

Much is going to depend on personal opinion, and argument is likely to fail at this point. The dilemma can be shown by quoting from two leading modern philosophers of religion. John Hick, in his book, *Arguments for the Existence of God*, says: "The atheistic option that the universe is 'just there' is the more economical option." Richard Swinburne, in his book, *The Existence of God*, says: "God is simpler than anything we can imagine and gives a simple explanation for the system." Your decision about which of these two views you favour will determine whether or not you find the Cosmological Argument persuasive.

If the Cosmological Argument succeeds, the uncaused cause, the unmoved mover, the being having of itself its own necessity, is clearly going to be the Thomist timeless God. This God is radically different from anything within the universe – nothing within the universe is the cause of itself and is dependent on nothing else. As we have already seen, it is very difficult to use language to talk about this timeless God, as this God is so different from us. God is so transcendent and unknowable that although we may be able to use language about God, we cannot really know what this language means. This is a necessary consequence of the timeless God view, and it is the price that supporters of timeless God have to pay for affirming God's transcendence and otherness.

Summary

The success of the Cosmological Argument depends first of all on a willingness to ask the question, "Why is there a universe?" If you are content to simply accept that the universe is there and does not need an explanation, or that it can be explained by an infinite regress, then the Cosmological Argument fails. In addition, God must also be shown to be a simpler or better ultimate explanation than the brute fact of the existence of the universe, and the idea of an uncaused cause which transcends the distinction between something and nothing must be shown to be credible.

NINE

The Ontological Argument

In the previous chapter we saw that the Cosmological Argument takes the existence of the universe as its starting point, and that it is therefore based on something which we experience – the universe.

The Ontological Argument is very different. Its starting point is with the definition of God. It attempts to prove that God exists by examining the definition of what God is. The Ontological Argument is, therefore, an *a priori argument*. (*A priori* arguments are those which are independent of experience – they do not in any way rely on experience as a starting point, but rather they rely on the analysis of an idea. For example, we do not have to meet or know any spinsters in order to understand that they must be female.) By understanding the definition of God we can come to see, it is held, that God exists.

The ways in which words are used in our language can provide us with information once we have understood what the words mean. When you have understood what it means to talk about a spinster, you will know that spinsters are always female and unmarried. This is what the word "spinster" means. By examining the subject of the sentence, "Spinsters are female and unmarried," we can see that the sentence is true. The predicates (or descriptions), "female" and "unmarried" are included within the definition of the word "spinster".

Philosophers differentiate between *synthetic* and *analytic* statements. A statement is synthetic if the predicate is not included in the subject. It is analytic if the predicate is included in the subject.

Take the following examples:

1.   (a) Spinsters are unmarried and female.
     (b) Triangles have three angles and three sides.

2.   (a) Spinsters are happy.
     (b) Triangles are the most common shape used in geometry.

Both statements 1.(a) and 1.(b) are analytic statements. We know they are true because the predicates (in (a) "unmarried and female" and in (b) "three angles and three sides") are included within the meaning of the subject (in (a) "spinsters" and in (b) "triangles").

However, we cannot know that 2.(a) and 2.(b) are true without research. Spinsters may be happy or they may not – we would have to interview many spinsters in order to find out. Triangles may be the most common figure in geometry or they may not – we would have to have evidence for this. They are both, therefore, synthetic statements – we cannot find out whether they are true just by understanding the meaning of words.

This brings us to the central question: *Is the statement, "God exists" a synthetic statement or an analytic one?*

The Ontological Argument maintains that "God exists" is analytically true. We can find out whether God exists by coming to understand the word "God". God cannot fail to exist.

The Cosmological Argument maintains that "God exists" is synthetically true. God may or may not exist – we have to find out whether or not He does exist by an argument which starts from some facts in the world that we experience. This was the approach that St Thomas Aquinas took, and he rejected the Ontological Argument. Aquinas also thought that we could not know what God was like in himself, and he maintained that people had very different ideas about God – both factors which made it impossible to arrive at God's existence by analysing the definition of God.

Saint Anselm, who was Archbishop of Canterbury from 1093 to 1109, thought that the Ontological Argument succeeded. He thought that God's existence could best be proved by analysing what it meant to talk about God.

Anselm's argument appears in his book called *Proslogion*, which is an address to God. This is important, and many commentators today do not recognise the context in which Anselm was putting forward the argument. Anselm believed in God and was reflecting on how self-evident the existence of God was to him – he was not trying to prove God's existence to someone who had no such belief.

If God's existence is going to be proved by looking at the definition of God, then this definition is obviously very important. Anselm defined God as "that than which no greater can be conceived." He claimed that something is more perfect or greater if it exists in reality rather than in our minds alone. An envelope containing a thousand pounds would be greater if it existed in my pocket rather than merely in my imagination! As God is defined as that than which no greater can be conceived, He must exist both in reality and in the mind.

At first sight this appears persuasive. After all, if we accept that once we know what a spinster is we can say she is unmarried, why cannot we similarly claim that once we understand what God is we can see that He must exist?

The monk Gaunilo replied to Anselm in his argument, *On behalf of the fool*. He asks us to imagine an island of such perfection that an island more perfect than it cannot be conceived. If this island is truly perfect, this perfection must include existence, as an existing island would be more perfect than a mere idea of the island in our minds. Therefore, Gaunilo claimed, if we follow Anselm's logic, the island must exist somewhere. Gaunilo is maintaining that we cannot define things into existence, and that we cannot show whether the island or God exists just by analysing an idea.

Anselm's reply to Gaunilo is important, as he effectively says, "Ah, but God is a special case." It is why God is a special case that makes the argument interesting today, and we shall return to this point shortly.

Rene Descartes put the Ontological Argument forward in a slightly different way. Descartes, like Anselm, maintained that existence cannot be separated from the idea of God. Just as once we understand what a triangle is we also understand that it necessarily has three sides, just as once we understand what a mountain is we also understand that it necessarily has a valley – so when we understand what God is we necessarily understand that God exists. We cannot think of a triangle without three sides – similarly we cannot understand what God is without accepting His existence.

David Hume's reply to this was that whatever can be thought of as existing can also be thought of as not existing. All propositions which deal with the existence of something ("God exists"; "unicorns exist"; "tables exist") can either be true or not true – in other words, they are synthetic. You cannot decide on the truth of any proposition about an object X by analysing X – which is what the Ontological Argument tries to do. X may or may not exist, but this cannot be determined by analysing X.

Kant's rejection of the Ontological Argument was similar. He rejected the whole idea of metaphysics and the attempt to get beyond the world of *phenomena* (the phenomenal world is the world as we experience it). He claimed that we cannot know what the world is like by any means which is independent of the way we experience the world. Kant also maintained that existence is not a predicate. We cannot make a long list of attributes and then add existence onto the end in order to bring the thing into reality. For example, the perfect car might have the following attributes:

(1)	(2)
Economical	Economical
Comfortable	Comfortable
Cheap to buy	Cheap to buy
Good performance	Good performance
Safe	Safe
Stereo system	Stereo system
Central door locking	Central door locking
Easy to service	Easy to service
Climate control	Climate control
Automatic braking system	Automatic braking system
Excellent styling	Excellent styling
Low wind resistance	Low wind resistance
Large carrying capacity	Large carrying capacity
	+ Existence

Kant was saying that we cannot make the theoretically ideal car into an existing ideal car simply by adding the word "exists" or "existence" to the specification. It would be marvellous if we could – you could draw up your description of the perfect husband or wife, add "and exists" to it, and then go out to look for him or her sure in the knowledge that he or she must exist! When we have a specification of anything, we have to go outside this specification to determine whether or not the thing exists. Kant says: "Whatever, therefore, and however much our concept of an object may contain, we must go outside it if we are to ascribe existence to the object."

Effectively Descartes and Anselm put forward two arguments:

1. The first argument holds that existence is a perfection or attribute. On this basis we could define the ideal car or the perfect island into existence. Just as being female is an attribute of being a spinster, so existing is an attribute of God.

   This simply does not work – the arguments of Gaunilo, Hume and Kant against this position are overwhelming.

2. God is a special case. God is unique and must exist. In his reply to Gaunilo, Anselm said: "If any man shall devise anything existing either in reality or in concept alone except that than which a greater cannot be conceived to which he can adapt the sequence of my reasoning, I will discover that thing, and will give him his lost island never to be lost again" (*Anselm's basic writings*, trans. Deane, p. 124). Only God has all perfections and the argument only applies to God.

Norman Malcolm ("Anselm's Ontological Argument", *The Philosophical Review*, 1960) drew attention to this distinction and it is very important. The Psalmist refers to the fool who says in his heart that there is no God. In fact the fool has not understood what it means to talk of God – just as the person who does not accept that a triangle has three angles has not understood what it means to talk of a triangle.

Once someone has understood what a triangle is, they will see that triangles have got to have three sides and three angles. Once someone has understood what a spinster is, they will see that spinsters have got to be female. Once someone has understood what it means to talk of prime numbers, they will see that prime numbers have got to exist. Similarly, once a person has understood what it means to talk of God, he or she will see that God must exist.

The crucial point here is what we mean by existence. Take the case of prime numbers, which we referred to in Chapter Seven. Once we have understood what prime numbers are, then prime numbers exist for us. A prime number is any number that is not divisible by any other number except itself and 1. That is what a prime number is. If you understand that, then you understand that prime numbers exist. However, it would be absurd to then ask, "Where is the prime number seven?" as though the perfect number seven was floating about in space somewhere! The very idea is nonsense. In fact, someone who asks such a question shows that he or she has not understood what a prime number is. Prime numbers certainly exist, but they exist because we have a use for the idea of prime numbers and because we understand how language about prime numbers is used. The statement, "Prime numbers exist" is true – and its truth depends simply on us understanding and having a use for language about prime numbers.

The same, in the anti-realist view, applies to the case of God, and this is what the second part of the Ontological Argument maintains. Once you have come to understand what "God" means, then God exists for you. The word "God" has meaning and value within the form of life of the religious believer. If you are a Christian, a Muslim or a Jew, then language about God has great meaning and value for you. For you and the members of your community it will be true that God does indeed exist.

This does *not*, however, mean that the word "God" refers to a timeless or spaceless creator of the universe. To think like this is simply – in this view – a mistake. Like language about prime numbers, language about God has meaning and value. The truth of the claim that God exists depends on its coherence with other true statements made by religious believers – it does *not* depend on reference to a creator God who is independent of the universe.

We can now see, therefore, why Aquinas was not persuaded by the Ontological Argument. He wanted to be able to say that there actually is a timeless creator God and that the statement, "God exists" is true because the word "God" refers to this creator. The Ontological Argument cannot prove this. The most it can do is to show that "God exists" is true within the form of life of the believing community. Aquinas, therefore, had to start his arguments from facts about the universe.

Summary

1. If the Ontological Argument seeks to prove that God exists as the creator and sustainer of the universe – whether as timeless substance or as an everlasting spirit – then it fails for the reasons given by Gaunilo, Aquinas, Hume and Kant.

2. If the Ontological Argument seeks to prove that, in the anti-realist revisionary view of God, God necessarily exists once a believer has come to understand what the word means, then the argument has considerable force. Once the believer understands what it means to talk of God, then God exists for him or her. God is a reality within the form of life of religious believers. The fool can only say in his heart that there is no God because he or she has not understood what it means to talk of God. Once he or she does understand what this talk means, he or she

will see that God necessarily exists, as talk about God has meaning and value for him or her. The truth of the statement, "God exists" does *not* depend on its correspondence to a being or spirit called God, but is rather based on the part the statement plays in the religious person's way of looking at and living in the world.

TEN

The Design Argument

The following extract is from a hymn by Paul Booth in BBC Radio for School's hymnbook *Come and Praise*:

> *Who put the colours in the rainbow?*
> *Who put the salt into the sea?*
> *Who put the cold into the snowflake?*
> *Who made you and me? . . .*
>
> *Who put the scent into the roses?*
> *Who taught the honey bee to dance?*
> *Who put the tree inside the acorn?*
> *It surely can't be chance.*

The idea that the universe "surely can't be chance" is at the root of the Design Argument for the existence of God. In the eighteenth century the scientific discoveries that were taking place seemed to be confirming more and more clearly the existence of God. The intricacies of the natural world and the way that the whole system of nature fitted together seemed clearly to point to the need for a great designer who had adapted trees, flowers, animals, microbes and fish to live together with the earth itself as a self-sustaining whole. This was an attractive picture, but it was criticised with devastating force by David Hume twenty-three years before the argument was put forward in its classical form by William Paley.

The Design Argument is not particularly Christian. It was

first recorded by Xenophon in 390 BC when he quoted Socrates as saying: "With such signs of forethought in the design of living creatures, can you doubt they are the work of choice or design?"

William Paley, the Archdeacon of Carlisle, developed the argument further. He argued that if someone walking across a heath were to come across a watch and then examine its workings, he or she would be strongly disposed to infer that there was a watchmaker who had made it. This would be the case even if the person were not entirely clear about the purpose of the watch. Clearly he or she would take it to be a complicated piece of machinery assembled by an intelligent being. Paley drew a parallel between the watch and God and said that the world, and indeed the human body, exhibits all the intricacies of a created whole, and that we are, therefore, entitled to infer a creator.

Hume, in Chapter XI of his *Dialogues Concerning Natural Religion* (published in 1719), forcefully criticised this argument. He used three characters – Cleanthes, Demea and Philo – to portray different positions. Philo, whose position is closest to Hume's own, is highly critical of the Design Argument, and his main criticisms can be summarised as follows:

1. If we argue that the order of creation is the work of a divine mind, then this mind itself must be complex, and we can ask who created this complex mind. Why, in other words, should we stop at God when asking for explanations?

2. The world contains much evil. If we are to argue from the facts in the world in order to arrive at the existence of God, if we take the facts seriously, we should end up with a God who is, at the least, not wholly good or, if he is

wholly good, is not powerful enough to bring his intentions about.

3. Why postulate one God as creator and not many? Many people contribute to the building of a ship. Perhaps many gods were involved in building the universe. What is more, once a man has made something, he may then leave his creation. Perhaps God has done the same, and this universe was only a practice attempt (and a poor one at that) by a trainee God. Hume puts this point as follows:

> The world, for aught the user of the design argument knows, is very faulty and imperfect, compared to a superior standard and was only the first rude effort of some infant Deity, who afterwards abandoned it, ashamed of his lame performance; it is the work of some dependent, inferior Deity; and is the object of derision to his superiors; it is the production of old age and dotage in some superannuated Deity, and ever since his death, has run on at adventures, from the first impulse and active force, which it received from him . . . (*Dialogues Concerning Natural Religion*, Ch. V).

Also, in humanity there are two sexes, so if we are to argue that like effects point to like causes, should we not argue for gods who are male and female and who reproduce? If we are really serious about drawing analogies between the manufacture of things in the world and the creation of the universe, should we not think in terms of gods who multiply and die on similar lines to ourselves?

4. The argument makes God very similar to a magnified human being – God ends up rather like a grander version of Superman.

5. We have no experience of universes being made. We cannot argue from causes operating within the universe to a cause of the whole universe.

Even if these problems could be overcome, Hume considers, we would still have to question the long and protracted time God took to bring his supposed purposes about. As he puts it:

> Look around this universe. What an immense profusion of beings . . . You admire this prodigious variety and fecundity. But inspect a little more narrowly these living creatures . . . How hostile and destructive to each other! How insufficient all of them for their own happiness! . . . The whole presents nothing but the idea of a blind nature, impregnated by a great vivifying principle, and pouring forth from her lap, without discernment or parental care, her maimed and abortive children.

Philo sums up Hume's view by saying:

> All religious systems are subject to great and insuperable difficulties. Each system exposes the absurdities, barbarities and pernicious tenets of its antagonists yet says It is right. All of them on the whole, prepare a complete triumph for the sceptic – a total suspension of judgement is our only reasonable recourse.

John Stuart Mill also challenged the Christian Argument from Design. Mill acknowledged that the argument might succeed in pointing to a God, but denied that it pointed to the Christian God. At the least, compromises would have to be made on God's attributes. If God were all-powerful, he could not be all-good. If he was all-good, he could not be all-powerful. In *Three Essays on Religion* Mill says:

Good
OLD
MILL

Next to the greatness of the cosmic forces is their perfect and absolute recklessness. They go straight to their end without regarding what or whom they crush on the road. Nearly all the things that men are hanged or imprisoned for doing to one another are nature's everyday performances. Nature kills at random and inflicts tortures in apparent wantonness. A hurricane destroys the hopes of a season, a flight of locusts or a flood desolates an area.

If the maker of the world can [do] all that he will, he wills misery, and there is no escaping that conclusion. Not even on the most twisted and distorted theory of good whichever was framed by religious and philosophic fanaticism can the government of nature be made to resemble the work of a God both good and omnipotent.

Hume's and Mill's attacks are powerful and important. When we looked at Stewart Sutherland's views in Chapter Six we saw that he rejects the traditional idea of a creator God because of the problem of evil, and he accuses believers of not starting with the facts. Sutherland is echoing the point made by both Hume and Mill. They all argue that if we start by looking at the way the world is – rather than with an unjustified assumption – we end up with an imperfect, a limited or a partly evil God. This need not necessarily be a problem. A number of modern theologians consider that God must be limited – although certainly not evil. They talk of a God who suffers with and through the universe. Such theologians are obviously thinking in terms of a temporal God. This is a God with whom it is relatively easy to identify, although some may hold that such a God is too limited to be worthy of worship.

A major event in the debate about the Design Argument was the discoveries of Darwin. Darwin's originality lay not in the theory of evolution, but in his suggesting a mechanism, *natural selection*, whereby new species could be formed from existing ones without the necessity for intervention by God. The hinge of a bivalve's shell need not, Darwin maintained, be made by an intelligent being in the way that a door hinge is made by man – the bivalve's hinge could have evolved naturally for a particular purpose.

Those who had supported the Design Argument had seen all the intricacies of nature as being the work of God. Darwin showed that natural selection, the survival of the fittest, could explain all the complexities. Natural selection was seen to conflict with Christianity in four main ways:

1. Genesis said that man had been created directly by God, so the accuracy of the Bible was called into question. The Roman Catholic encyclical *Humanae Generis* (August 1950) condemned the denial of Adam's existence as a historical person, and also the denial that original sin reached us by direct descent from him, and the denial that the soul was not created directly by God.

2. Genesis pictured man falling from grace into a state of sin. Darwin pictured man evolving into rationality.

3. Genesis said that God had created man in his own image, whereas natural selection maintained that man's higher faculties had evolved naturally.

4. In general, natural selection was considered to undermine the Argument from Design because it was a mechanism that could explain what had previously been considered to be the handiwork of God.

In the years after Darwin published his findings, tens of thousands of Christians left their churches because they could no longer believe in God. Today, almost all Christians accept natural selection and do not find this in any way incompatible with belief in God. It can be argued that natural selection itself might be the mechanism that God uses to bring about His purposes. Darwin recognised that natural selection did not explain everything. For example, man's moral faculties and the way human beings care for weak members of their species and are willing to sacrifice their own lives for others seem hard to explain if natural selection is the only mechanism at work. Darwin himself said: "It is extremely doubtful if the offspring of more benevolent parents would be reared in greater numbers than the children of selfish parents" (quoted in David Lack's *Evolutionary Theory and Christian Belief*).

If the survival of the fittest really is the motive force for the development of the human moral sense, then it seems hard to explain the fact that we take care of the handicapped and mentally retarded and allow people who have genetic defects to have children. An attitude based on the survival of the fittest would say that such individuals lower the quality of the human gene pool and should therefore be eliminated. And yet, by and large, our society cares for its weak members. A proposal to compulsorily sterilise anyone with an I.Q. of under 100 (which, in theory, should improve the intelligence of the population over a number of generations) would fill most people with horror.

F. R. Tennant has presented the Design Argument in a revised form. He maintains that theism is the most probable world hypothesis and uses an extended Design Argument which takes Darwin into account. He sees the fact of natural selection as being fully in accordance with divine purpose on a grand scale. The whole evolutionary process can be seen to be the work of God. Thus:

The fitness of the world to be the home of living beings

92

depends on certain primary conditions – astronomical, thermal, chemical, etc. and on the coincidence of qualities, apparently not causally connected with each other. The unique assembly of unique properties on so vast a scale makes the organic world comparable to an organism. It is suggestive of a formative principle.

The world is compatible with a single throw of dice and common sense is not foolish in suspecting the dice to have been loaded. —

In other words Tennant is maintaining that God arranged the whole universe to provide the conditions necessary for life to evolve. Evolution can, therefore, be seen as part of God's plan.

Tennant also develops an *aesthetic argument*, based on the presence of beauty in the world. Beauty, music and the appreciation of art cannot, he claims, be shown to have any useful part to play in evolution or the survival of the fittest. Thus he says:

Nature is not just beautiful in places, it is saturated with beauty – on the telescopic and microscopic scale. Our scientific knowledge brings us no nearer to understanding the beauty of music. From an intelligibility point of view, beauty seems to be superfluous and to have little survival value . . .

Both of Tennant's arguments are attractive, but we also need to take into account the horrific suffering in Stalin's, Nazi Germany's and Pol Pot's death camps; the starvation of those afflicted by poor harvests in the third world; the pain caused by cancer; natural disasters such as earthquakes, tidal waves and volcanic eruptions; the suffering caused by loneliness and the misery endured by people all over the world.

To be sure, certain of these ills can be blamed on human beings, but others cannot. An all-powerful, all-loving God could have created a world in which earthquakes and small-pox did not occur. Smallpox has now been eradicated, but why was it necessary for it to exist in the first place?

Basil Mitchell (in *The Justification for Religious Belief*, Macmillan 1973) puts forward a cumulative case for belief in God. Richard Swinburne (in *The Existence of God*, Oxford 1979) argues for a probability approach. Both employ modified versions of the Design Argument and try to show that *theism* (belief in God) makes better sense of all the evidence that we have available than any alternative. Swinburne says there are two types of Design Argument:

1. *Teleological arguments* – arguments which start from a general pattern of order in the universe, and
2. *Arguments from providence* – arguments which start from the provision for the needs of temporal beings (animals, humans, etc.).

Swinburne concentrates on the first of these. He is not primarily concerned with spatial order – such as the adaptation of birds and bees to the air, fish to the sea and man to the world. He feels that the great strength of the Design Argument lies in the *temporal order* of the universe. It is the orderliness of the universe that he finds so very remarkable – its conformity to simple, scientific laws which provide the conditions necessary for life. Thus:

1. Universal orderliness reigns over distances of billions of light years, and science cannot explain why all bodies possess the same powers and abilities and conform to the same laws. Such an explanation is too big for science, which has to assume the existence of natural laws and work within them.

94

2. The universe might have been chaotic, but it is in fact very orderly.

The universe is like a machine-making machine. We have experience of these. God, Swinburne claims, made a "do-it-yourself-kit" world – a world which human beings are free to improve or to harm, within narrow limits. The existence of orderliness and uniform natural laws suggests that the universe was designed for this purpose. It is more probable than not that the natural laws were designed – hence God's existence is more probable than not.

[handwritten margin note: HOW DOES HE KNOW THIS]

Swinburne assumes, without argument, that human beings are the highest things in creation and the reason for the universe being as it is. However, this may be an unwarranted assumption. The dinosaurs were wiped out – we are still not entirely sure why or how – and their existence seems to have contributed little or nothing to the development of human beings. Perhaps human beings will also be wiped out so that a new form of life will be able to emerge from the ruins we leave behind. As Gaskin puts it:

> We ourselves may just as easily be an expendable stage on the way to some other divine purpose . . . As far as the natural facts of evolution are concerned, it is pure prejudice to portray *our* intelligence as like to God's, rather than God's as like to something else – we know not what – which will be the final end and outcome of the divine purpose being expressed in evolution.
>
> (*The Quest for Eternity*, Pelican, 1984, p. 72)

Swinburne's argument, therefore, contains a hidden assumption – as do all forms of the Design Argument.

To those who say that there is too much suffering in the world to justify belief in an omnipotent and all-good God,

Swinburne replies that their demand is for a "toy world", a world where nothing matters very much. If we are to have the higher virtues, if we are to learn and to develop our do–it–yourself–kit world, then pain and suffering are necessary. If there were no death, there could be no murder, but neither could there be birth or any ultimate self-sacrifice. Swinburne also says that God has set limits to the amount of human suffering. Human beings pass out when pain passes a certain point, and death provides a sure end to all suffering. This is an indication of the compassion of a creator God.

I have to say that when I think of the extreme torture inflicted by some governments upon their opponents, or of the pain of a child dying of throat cancer, or of the anguish of a mother watching her baby die of starvation, this latter argument leaves me nearly speechless! However, perhaps I am too tender-hearted. The reader must make his or her own judgement.

The critic could reply to Swinburne's more general argument by saying that the existence of raw matter and the fundamental laws that govern matter may be the ultimate brute fact, just as God is assumed by the theist to be the ultimate brute fact. Also, the argument from natural order gives no indication of benevolence or goodness, just evidence of a good designer who is not particularly interested in human beings (given the amount of pain and suffering in the world) and that, of course, takes us back to the arguments of Hume and Mill.

The Duke of Argyle recorded a conversation he had with Darwin during the last year of the scientist's life. The Duke said to Darwin that it was impossible not to construe a designer from the works of nature. Darwin apparently looked at him very hard and said: "Well, that often comes over me with overwhelming force, but at other times" – he shook his head vaguely – "it seems to go away."

The Jesuit poet Gerard Manley Hopkins starts his poem, *God's Grandeur* with the line "The world is charged with the grandeur of God." This, however, may tell us more about the way Hopkins looked at the world than about whether or not God exists as, in any sense, an agent who created and sustains the universe.

If the Design Argument succeeds, it points to a God who is in some ways like a superhuman person. The argument rests on there being parallels between human design within the universe and the divine design of the universe as a whole. The God that is implied by the argument is closest to the everlasting model. Such a God may well be limited and suffer with and through creation, as some modern theologians maintain (Moltmann is a good example). This is, of course, a realist view – in this view statements about God are held to correspond to the designer God who created the universe. The argument could also point to the timeless God, but there are fewer parallels between such a God and human designers, so the force of the argument is reduced.

Summary

1. If the Design Argument is to be taken seriously it must recognise the facts about the world from which it is working. These facts include natural selection; the presence of great beauty; the higher human capacities, such as love, unselfishness and morality; the pain and suffering which human beings cause one another; the suffering of animals and the suffering due to natural disasters which are beyond the control of human beings.

2. If the argument is to succeed, these facts must point to a God who, if He is the traditional Christian, Jewish or Muslim God, must be *omnipotent* (all-powerful), *omni-*

scient (all-knowing) and *wholly good*. We shall define these terms with greater precision later in the book. Some modern theologians have supported the idea of a limited and suffering God, and this approach might well be supported by the Design Argument. For the moment, the reader must decide whether the facts we know about the world make the existence of such a God more probable or not.

3.   The argument rests on probability and individual judgement. It is not, therefore, going to be conclusive, and much will depend on each individual's reaction to it. Philosophically this sort of value judgement is not easy to justify, and the argument may owe more to its persuasive power than to its logic.

ELEVEN

The Argument from Religious Experience

It was late that Sunday evening and the disciples were gathered together behind locked doors, because they were afraid of the Jewish authorities. Then Jesus came and stood among them. "Peace be with you," he said. After saying this he showed them his hands and his side . . .

One of the twelve disciples, Thomas (called the twin), was not with them when Jesus came. So the other disciples told him, "We have seen the Lord." Thomas said to them, "Unless I see the scars of the nails in his hands and put my finger in those scars and my hand in his side, I will not believe."

(John 20:19–24)

We have here the classic religious experience, and the response which typically accompanies it. A small group of people have a religious experience, but their reports are not believed. As it was in St Thomas' time, so it has been for nearly two thousand years. Many individuals and groups have claimed many different types of religious experience – some people have accepted their reports but many others have been sceptical. We have, therefore, to consider whether religious experiences can provide a fountain for faith or the basis for an argument for the existence of God.

It is all too easy to talk of religious experience in general, but there are many different types. Richard Swinburne (in *The Existence of God*) provides a helpful analysis. He defines five different types of religious experiences – two are public, in that they can be seen by anyone who is present, whilst three are individual and private.

Public experiences

1. An individual sees God or God's action in a public object or scene. However, the purported religious experience can readily be explained on other grounds.

    For instance, the believer might look at the night sky and see the hand of God, whilst the non-believer might just see a beautiful sunset. In this case a great deal depends on personal interpretation.

2. Very unusual public events occur, involving a breach of natural law.

    Examples might include someone walking on water or a person appearing in a locked room or water turning into wine. There is less emphasis on personal interpretation here, although the sceptic can still maintain that whilst something inexplicable may have occurred, there is no need to attribute this to God. A hundred years ago a video camera might have been considered miraculous, whereas today it is simply an example of modern technology.

Private experiences

By their very nature, these are less easily verified than public experiences:

3. Experiences which an individual can describe using normal language.

    Examples might include Jacob's vision of a ladder going up to heaven or the appearance of the Angel Gabriel to Mary. There is, of course, always a problem with the interpretation of dreams – and many would look for psychological rather than divine explanations of them.

4. Experiences which cannot be described in normal language but which are nevertheless very real to those experiencing them.

   Mystical experiences are the most obvious examples of this category. The mystic may be the first to admit that normal language is not adequate to express what has happened. These experiences may be of great intensity and may be of various types. Often the mystic will resort to contradictions in order to try to express himself. For example: "Black did not cease to be black, nor white cease to be white, but black became white and white became black."

5. In this case, there is no specific experience, but the individual feels that God is acting in his or her life. Looking back on past events, the individual may say, "God's hand guided me" – although if pressed he or she would admit that there is no specific evidence for this.

Swinburne's analysis suffers from the defect of making religious experiences appear very similar to ordinary experiences. He has little feeling for what Otto described as "the numinous" or "an apprehension of the wholly other". Nevertheless, the analysis is helpful in that it forces us to be clearer about which sort of experience we are referring to when discussing the Argument from Religious Experience.

Swinburne maintains that we should rely on reports of religious experience because of two central principles which, he claims, are fundamental aspects of rationality.

The principle of credulity

[handwritten: ? The sun seems to circle the earth. But it does]

How things seem to be is a good guide to how things are.
From this it would follow that in the absence of special
considerations, all religious experiences are to be taken by
their subjects to be substantial grounds for belief in the
existence of their apparent object – God, or Mary, or
Ultimate Reality or Poseidon . . .

If it seems . . . to a subject that X is present, then
probably X is present; what one seems to perceive is
probably so.

(*The Existence of God*, p. 270)

At first glance this appears reasonable. In the absence of
evidence to the contrary, we should trust that what appears to
be the case is in fact so. However, in the case of religious
experience the issue is much more contentious than this.

The principle of testimony

Swinburne's second principle claims that in the absence of
evidence to the contrary, we should rely on the reports of
experiences which we hear. *[handwritten: How would we know that the reports weren't lies?]*

In the absence of special considerations the experiences of
others are (probably) as they report them . . . In general
there are no special considerations for doubting what subjects report about their religious experiences (p. 272).

Swinburne claims that it is reasonable to accept that other
people normally tell the truth. So, in the absence of special
considerations, it is reasonable to believe the reports of those
who claim to have had religious experiences.

Swinburne's arguments have been helpfully built upon and

reinforced by Caroline Davis (*The Evidential Force of Religious Experience*, Oxford, 1989). I will be bringing their combined approaches together here – although, obviously, I cannot do justice to their arguments, particularly those of Davis, in the space here available.

Swinburne's two principles seem attractive, but I think his position is a good deal less straightforward than it is made to appear. It may be helpful to draw a parallel with the claimed sighting of UFOs (Unidentified Flying Objects). Great numbers of people have claimed to have seen UFOs. Many people in many different countries have claimed to have seen flying saucers, little green men, spaceships, strange happenings, circles on the ground and so on. However, most of us are rightly sceptical about such claims.

If I thought I could see a flying saucer in the sky, I would be extremely dubious about it. I would try to think of other possible explanations. Perhaps it might be a meteorological balloon, or an experimental plane, a hang glider seen from an odd angle, with the light playing tricks on my eyes. Also, perhaps I might have been to a particularly good party, or there might even be something wrong with my eyes. In addition I would seek confirmation from radar stations and from other people who might have seen it. I would do all this before admitting that what I saw was, indeed, a flying saucer. I agree that if the evidence were overwhelming, then I would have to accept it. If I saw the flying saucer land in my garden; if I went out to it and touched it; if I met the little green men who got out of it, and they invited me in for a cup of coffee, then I would have to accept that I had, indeed, seen a flying saucer. Experience of unusual objects can be veridical, but I would have to be very sure indeed about the experience before accepting that it was indeed what it appeared to me to be. I do not think this makes me unduly sceptical – just cautious about such an odd experience.

The same could apply if I were driving close to Loch Ness and thought I saw the monster. I know many people have claimed to see Nessie, but sometimes their reports have been discredited, as they have been shown to be based on faked photographs. Sometimes they may have been genuinely mistaken. Extensive searches for the monster, using the latest equipment, have failed to produce any results. I am, therefore, going to be a sceptic about monster sightings – even my own – unless I am presented with incontrovertible evidence. In this my position seems very similar to that of Jesus' disciple, Thomas.

I suggest that there are parallels between claims to religious experience, claims to UFO sightings and claims to have seen the Loch Ness monster. The probability of all such experiences seems to be low, and therefore the quality of the claimed experiences must be proportionately high. A good case can be made, in theory, for the existence of alien civilisations. There are billions of stars and the chances are high that some of these will have planetary systems where life may have developed. It is entirely possible that these civilisations may be much older and more advanced than ours and that they may have visited us. However, my acceptance of this theoretical possibility will not prevent me being sceptical about UFO sightings.

Davis questions my scepticism about applying the Principle of Credulity to religious experiences. She examines a whole range of possible challenges to the accuracy of such experiences. She maintains that, while some challenges may have force, the balance of probability rests with religious experiences pointing beyond themselves to something that has actually been experienced. She draws on psychology, philosophy, theology and religious studies to present a cumulative case which, she argues, is convincing and which takes account of the most obvious challenges – such as that religious experiences are due to psychological states, or that they should be dismissed because they are relative to different cultures (for example, Catholics tend to experience the Virgin Mary and Evangelical Christians "the risen Lord Jesus", whilst Hindus, Muslims and Buddhists tend to have experiences from within their own traditions).

I do not have space to examine Davis' arguments here, but they seem to be reasonably convincing *if* – and it is a big if – the probability of God's existence is reasonably strong. Davis might well have added to her argument the research work of David Hay at the Oxford Centre for Religious Experience. Hay has conducted many interviews throughout the country under carefully controlled conditions and has found (as recorded in his book, *Inner Space*) that a very high proportion of people claim to have had experiences of a power or presence beyond themselves.

If one is an unbiased observer with no preconceptions, then claims to religious experiences or sightings of UFOs or the Loch Ness monster will, in my view, all be treated with scepticism. If, of course, I am already a believer, then I will be much more inclined to accept experiences that tend to confirm my beliefs, but in this case the beliefs predate the experiences and the experiences do not provide a foundation for belief.

Swinburne and Davis claim that the Religious Experience Argument for the existence of God succeeds only as part of an overall probability-type approach. I agree with them on this.

Swinburne's method in his book is to examine the different arguments for the existence of God and, in so doing, he comes to the conclusion that God's existence is not improbable. He then, in his final chapter, throws all the weight on the Argument from Religious Experience which, he considers, makes the existence of a personal God of infinite capacities a simpler explanation for the existence of the universe than any rival hypothesis. Swinburne does not, however, develop the Argument from Religious Experience fully, and it is here that Davis comes in.

Davis accepts the broad structure of Swinburne's argument and says:

> If the evidence other than religious experience does not show theism to be improbable, then the evidence of the many religious experiences which escape pathological and other challenges will be sufficient to make some relatively unramified theistic claims probable (p. 235).

Davis argues that neither the conflicting claims of different religious experiences within various religious traditions nor the challenges of those who seek to explain claims to religious experiences in psychological or other natural terms are sufficient to undermine the claims to authenticity made by religious believers. She says:

> In particular, numinous and mystical experiences and senses of a "presence" provide very strong evidence for broadly theistic beliefs. These include the claims that human beings have a "'true self" beyond their everyday "phenomenal ego" and that this true self is intimately related to the divine nature; that there is a holy power beyond the world of the senses . . . and that human beings can find their most profound satisfaction in a harmonious relation with this holy power (p. 238).

These claims are very substantial indeed and, if they could be justified, then religious believers would indeed be able to rely on religious experience – seen as part of a cumulative case – as a foundation for belief in God.

The starting points of both Swinburne and Davis can be

challenged. For example, neither thinker takes seriously enough the problem of evil. Davis maintains that there are many reasonable explanations for the existence of evil, although she does not have space to examine these. I believe she is too sanguine about this. The challenges put forward by Hume and Mill (which were covered in the previous chapter) are very real indeed. I am far from persuaded that any of the potential explanations are convincing.

The problem is that an assessment of probability is an individual matter and rests on an individual value judgement. You may weigh all the evidence and come to the conclusion that belief in God is not at all probable, while I may weigh the same evidence and come to the conclusion that it is probable. It is not easy to assume an unbiased starting point in order to determine who is right.

There are two basic difficulties. First, in the case of the individual who has the experience, how does one separate:

1.   "God appeared to me last night" from
2.   "It seemed to me that God appeared to me last night"?

Secondly, in the case of the person who is told about the experience, how does one separate:

1.   "God appeared to him or her last night" from
2.   "He or she thought that God appeared to him or her last night"?

Even if the individual who has the experience is satisfied about its veracity, should others be convinced by his or her report? Innumerable people throughout the world report many strange experiences – they experience Gods, aliens, monsters, witches, vampires, demons, devils, ghosts, spirits and saints. Who does the uncommitted observer believe?

The Argument from Religious Experience is, I suggest, going to depend to a very large extent on one's presuppositions. If one's presuppositions favour particular types of experiences, one is likely to be convinced by reports of them. If one is a sceptic one will need a great deal of convincing.

If we take as an example St Paul's experience on the Damascus road (surely the best known of all religious experiences), we note that the three accounts of the experience given in the Acts of the Apostles differ quite markedly (chapters 9, 22 and 26). Millions have found Paul's accounts persuasive – millions more have not. There are, of course, some tests that can be applied to any claim to a religious experience. For instance, we can ask whether the experience has had a major influence on the life of the person claiming it. Or we can ask whether it fits in with other things we claim to know from within our tradition – but by referring to our tradition we are already bringing our own preconceptions to bear on the matter.

Religious experiences normally occur within faith rather than act as a foundation for faith. I accept that for the individual a particularly vivid experience may constitute a turning point in his or her life. This certainly happened to St Paul. Many others, however, saw Jesus and chose to ignore his message. Someone's claim to have had a religious experience should properly be met by a great deal more scepticism than Swinburne or Davis allow for. The creator God may well exist and some people may indeed experience His loving presence, but there seems no convincing reason why others should accept their reports. A more effective testimony than the report of the experiences would be the transformation that should, if the experience was true, take place in the individual's life. Such a transformation may indeed be inspiring and may cause others to reappraise their own lives and to live and act in a different way. But a transformation in a human life does not prove that God exists – only that the Danish philosopher Kierkegaard was right in saying that people are free and can always surprise us.

God may or may not exist. We must decide this question for ourselves, and we must also decide what we think this claim means. Some people will undoubtedly be convinced by religious experiences, while others will not. It seems unjust to say that one group is less rational or more hard-hearted than another. They may simply start from different positions.

Of course, if there is a God who does appear directly or indirectly to individuals, then this is going to be either the timeless or the everlasting God. Interestingly, Nicholas Lash in his book, *Easter in Ordinary* (SCM, 1988), although affirming a creator God, rejects the possibility of this God appearing in any extraordinary way to human beings. Lash says that God is instead to be found in the ordinary things in life. If Lash is right – and I am not at all sure that he is – this places even greater weight on the individual's interpretation of his or her experience and hence, again, on his or her existing presuppositions.

I am not convinced, therefore, that reports of religious experiences (to be contrasted with religious experiences which you or I may have personally) provide a sound foundation for faith. You, of course, may feel differently. That is the problem – individual preconceptions differ.

Summary

Reports of religious experiences may point to the existence of a creator God if the existence of such a God is, in the absence of such reports, not improbable. Whether it is seen to be improbable or not will depend to a great extent upon individual presuppositions.

TWELVE

Omnipotence

God's omnipotence is one of the facets of the Rubik cube of God. It is important to understand which meaning of the word "omnipotence" each different model of God will tolerate. We need to separate the realist views of God, which maintain that God is the creator and sustainer of the universe, from the revisionary views which do not see God in these terms.

The realist view – God as everlasting or timeless

Religious believers say that God is almighty. By this they mean that He can do anything. Believers are obviously anxious that God's providential care for them should not be in any way limited by lack of power. Certain of Jesus' miracles were specifically intended to show that, like God, he too had power over the physical universe – he changed water into wine and "even the winds and the waves obeyed him".

However, once we start to examine the claim that God can do anything, we encounter some complications. These complications are not just the province of philosophers interested in picking holes in religious belief – almost all teenagers who have any interest in religion will be aware of them. Some examples will show the problems which are involved. They are examples which most readers will find familiar, as they probably heard them during their school days:

1. If God can do anything, can he commit suicide?

2. Can God swim? My six-year-old daughter can swim, so if God cannot do so, this seems a clear limitation to His power.

3. Can God sin? Many of us do this all the time, so if God can do everything, He should be able to do this as well.

4. Can God make an object which is too heavy for Him to lift? I can do this with the aid of a concrete mixer, some sand and some cement, but it would seem that whatever answer we give in the case of God necessarily limits His power. If He cannot create such an object, then He cannot do something that a human being can do. But if He can create such a thing, then there is something that He cannot do – namely, lift the object.

5. Can God make an object so that it is completely black all over and at the same time white all over? Alternatively, can God make a square circle?

These challenges to the idea that God can do anything are highly significant – particularly to the realists who maintain that there is a God who created the world and who interacts with it. We shall have to develop a definition of omnipotence which can take these problems into account. We shall go through various possibilities:

Definition One: God can do absolutely anything – including the logically impossible.

On this view, God can do all of the above. He can do things which are contradictory, He can do the nonsensical. He can create square circles, commit suicide and swim. He can even make a stone which is too heavy for Him to lift – *and then go on to lift it!* God is not limited by the laws of logic, since He created these laws and could abolish them if he wished to do so.

The French philosopher Rene Descartes maintained this position, and it is the strongest affirmation of God's power. Descartes considered that if God had to conform to the laws of logic and non-contradiction, this would be a limit on His absolute power. This is an approach that is sometimes taken by believers who have never really thought through the problems that arise. Such individuals need to take seriously the fact that even the Bible accepts that there are things that God cannot do – it says that God is not able to lie or to swear by a being greater than Himself (Hebrews 6:13,18).

The view that God can do the logically impossible is incoherent and, if it were true, would show that God could be fundamentally evil. Such a God could lie and deceive – he could swear to reward the virtuous and then condemn them to everlasting torment. Duplicity would be part of God's essential character. Even if such a view were possible, this could not be a God worth worshipping.

Logic and the laws of contradiction mark the limits to what it makes sense to say. It is meaningless to talk of square circles. Nothing could be a square circle – if it was a square it would not be a circle and if it was a circle it would not be a square. It is true, of course, that God could arrange some strange geometric figure and call this a square circle, but He would then be making up a private language of His own – certainly He would not have created what we mean by a square circle. This, however, is no limitation on His power.

Even more telling than this, however, is the fact that a God who could do the logically impossible would be funda- mentally evil. This can be shown by the following argument.

One of the most effective arguments to justify belief in an

all-good and all-powerful God in the face of much evil and suffering in the world is the *free will defence*. This argument claims that God allows human beings free will in order that they may be free to love Him and to show love to their neighbours. Love requires freedom; love is only possible if freedom exists. A person who is not free is unable to love. A robot could mimic the actions of love, but this would not be the same as genuine love.

Therefore, if human beings are to love they must be free, and if they are free they have to have the power to be free to choose to do dreadful things on some occasions. Events such as the slaughter of the Poles, the Gipsies and the Jews in the Nazi concentration camps, the killings in Stalin's death camps and the massacres carried out by the Pol Pot regime in Cambodia are all examples of human free will being used to inflict massive suffering. The free will defence maintains that God could not interfere to stop these tragedies without taking away human freedom. Human freedom is such an important gift from God that the price of suffering is held to be worth it. Only if we are free can we enter into love-relationships with each other and with God.

However, if God could do the logically impossible, as Descartes claimed, then He could bring about two mutually contradictory states of affairs. God could have created a world such that:

1. Human beings would have the genuine free will that they now possess, *and*
2. These free beings could be controlled in such a way that they would only act justly, kindly and rightly.

Now these two positions are contradictories. A person cannot *both* be completely free to choose how he or she will act *and at the same time* be controlled so that he or she always acts rightly. The two cannot go together – that would amount to logical nonsense. If, however, God can do the logically impossible, then there would be no problem in Him doing the logically nonsensical. According to this view of omnipotence, God *could* have created this ideal state of affairs (Ninian Smart refers to it as "the Utopian Thesis") whereby complete freedom and goodness would be combined. God's failure to bring about this state of affairs shows that He must be malevolent and, effectively, playing with human beings. All the evils that men have inflicted on other men and women could have been avoided, and at no cost.

However, because God cannot do the logically impossible this is an impossible state of affairs. God could *either* control us so that we would act rightly, in which case we would not be free, *or* He could give us freedom, in which case human evil must be permitted. Therefore we need another definition of omnipotence.

Definition Two: God can do everything that is logically possible.

This seems attractive, but this definition of omnipotence is not adequate either. The examples given at the beginning of the chapter illustrate the problems. It is certainly logically possible for my six-year-old daughter to swim, but if God is timeless and has not got a body this is likely to be impossible for him – although, of course, Jesus may well have swum in the lake when he was a child. (This raises questions as to whether it is logically possible for a literally timeless God to become a human being. However, such questions would involve us discussing Christology, and we do not have space for that here.) It is certainly logically possible for a human person to commit suicide or to sin, just as it is logically possible to make an object which is too heavy to lift.

If, therefore, we define omnipotence as "the power to do everything that is logically possible", then God will have to be able to do things which the believer often wants to say He cannot do (like doing evil, lying, committing suicide or even committing adultery). <u>A further modification of the definition is, therefore, required.</u>

Definition Three: God can do everything that it is logically possible for Him to do.

At first, this may seem to be the same as Definition Two. However, there is a crucial additional modification. This definition is effectively saying that God can do anything that is logically possible for Him, given His nature, to do.

Anthony Kenny, in *The God of The Philosophers* (p. 98) expresses this definition of omnipotence with greater precision. He says:

> Divine omnipotence, therefore, if it is to be a coherent notion, must be something less than the complete omnipotence which is the possession of all logically possible powers. It must be a narrower omnipotence, consisting in the possession of all logically possible powers which it is logically possible for a being with the attributes of God to possess.

This is a very attractive possibility. Much will, of course, depend on what is meant by God's nature. If God is timeless substance His nature will be different to what it will be if He is an everlasting spirit. On this view, God can do anything which is (1) logically possible and (2) in accordance with His nature.

If God is timeless substance then, as we have seen, He cannot be other than He is. Time does not pass for God and God is metaphysically perfect – no change at all is possible. It follows, therefore, that it would be logically impossible for such a God to commit suicide, as this would involve Him ceasing to exist. Since this would amount to a change in God, it would not be a possible state of affairs. Suicide would, therefore, be logically impossible for God (although not for a human person), as it would involve a change which would go against God's nature. Similarly, we can say that it would be logically impossible for God to swim (although not for my six-year-old daughter), since swimming is a temporal activity and God is timeless.

Whether timeless God can sin or not depends on how we define sin. Protestants tend to think of sin in terms of a breach of the relationship that the believer has with God. Of course, God could not breach a relationship with Himself. The everlasting God could, however, choose to perform acts that we would regard as evil – although then one could either say that God would never do such acts or that such acts, if done by God, would not be evil. Neither view would limit the claim that God was omnipotent.

Aquinas and the Catholic Church have tended to define sin as a falling short of goodness. This effectively amounts to saying that we, as human beings, sin when we fall short of our true human nature. If this definition is accepted, sin becomes logically impossible for timeless God, He cannot be other than He is. God cannot, logically, fall short of the true perfection of his nature, as this would involve a change, and timeless God cannot change.

If God is an everlasting spirit, then time does pass for Him. Because of this such a God *could* change. On this basis, it is logically possible for Him to commit suicide, and it would also be logically possible for Him to sin. Neither statement, of course, implies that God *would* sin or that he *would* commit suicide, but this would be a matter of His free choice, not of constraints imposed by His nature. An everlasting spirit does not have a body, so it would not be possible for such a God to swim – unless, of course, He was to take a body, as happened, advocates of this view would argue, in the case of Jesus.

This definition of omnipotence is coherent and plausible, but it suffers from one disadvantage. It does not necessarily say a great deal. Imagine a person who suffered from some disease, so that he could not perform any voluntary action at all except blink his eyes. Imagine that the physical defects that prevented other actions were irreversible and that this individual's very nature was limited to performing this one action. On the basis of the definition given in this section, this person would be omnipotent, as he could do all those things which it is logically possible for a person having his nature to do. Since the only thing his nature permitted him to do was to blink his eyes, he would be omnipotent, since that was what he could do! Much will depend, on this view, on how we define a person's nature – and critics of the example I have just given might well say that no person's nature could ever be so confined that he could only blink. Some other human potentialities would still remain.

The definition, "God can do everything that it is logically possible for Him to do" is, therefore, the most coherent and plausible of the alternatives. However, the constraints imposed by God's nature will determine what is and what is not possible for Him to bring about as a result of His omnipotent power.

Revisionary approaches to talk about God

We have looked in previous chapters at four different views of God. Two of these views were realist claims, in that they maintained that God exists independently of the universe He created. One claimed that God was timeless substance and the other that God was an everlasting spirit. In both cases, talk of God's omnipotence was talk about the power of these Gods to

act, and in the discussion above we have explored a convincing way of understanding this omnipotence.

However, two other views of God remain open. The first is
the realist claim put forward by Sutherland that talk about
God is talk about a possible way of living life, whilst the
second is the anti-realist claim which sees God as a reality
within the form of life of religious believers. Both deny that
God is in any sense an agent. It might seem, therefore, that
both these two views would dismiss talk of God's omnipotence, but this is not the case.

To talk of God's omnipotence, on these views, is to show
that a different way of living life is possible and that this life
can provide a triumph over adversity of every sort. It is
possible to live life in such a way that any individual can
overcome the trivialisation of his or her life.

The lover of the good cannot be harmed. This means that
nothing can take away from him or her the inner orientation
towards kindness, love and virtue which is the most important part of his or her life. To be sure, such individuals can
lose possessions and suffer pain and even death, but since the
most important thing in their lives is the way they live and the
path of holiness that they follow, they cannot really be hurt in
any important sense.

Although Sutherland did not do so, he might well have
drawn on an example like Gandhi here. Gandhi showed that
the path of peace, the refusal of violence, is a path that can
overcome all opposition. Gandhi himself was killed, but his
killer could not overcome the life and example he showed to
human beings. The Anglican Archbishop of Uganda, killed
by Idi Amin, in the end helped to defeat the general by his
example and by the inspiration which he gave to Christians in
the country. Nelson Mandela, locked up for over twenty-five
years by the South African government on Robbin Island,
and released in 1990 became a recognised international figure

and a key element in the future of his country, in spite of having no power and being completely subject to the South African authorities. Similarly, the might and power of the Warsaw Pact and the control exercised by Stalinist communism over so many millions in Eastern Europe was overcome not by force of arms, but by largely peaceful and popular movements.

Kruschev is said to have asked, "How many divisions has the Pope?" as a way of mocking the powerlessness of the Church. And yet it is the Church that in country after country around the world provides the inspiration for the poor and the weak and helps to bring about a more equal and fair society. Sutherland probably did not make use of such examples because, for him, the real omnipotence which accompanies the life of holiness is an inner orientation which does not depend on how things go in the world. Death can be overcome because, if we will only follow the path of holiness, death cannot trivialise our lives. Sutherland would be reluctant to measure omnipotence in external terms. This is a fair point, and possibly both ways of understanding omnipotence are, in their different ways, legitimate.

It is in these senses that the path of sanctity can be the path of omnipotence. Even if people die in a just cause, they have overcome death, as their lives have not been rendered meaningless by their passing away.

Omnipotence, therefore, in both the realist and anti-realist revisionary accounts of Christianity, does not need to be the power exercised by a God who created the world and who still controls it. Rather, talk of omnipotence seeks to draw people to the invincible power of love which is found in weakness, in humility and in selflessness. Such an omnipotence can be enjoyed by the poorest of the poor, but not by the rich – they have too much to lose. Their possessions get in between them and the Kingdom of God, just as the possessions of the rich young man in the Christian Gospels prevented him from following Jesus. The Kingdom of God is to be built on earth, and the builders are those who seek to live out lives of love in the midst of a world dedicated largely to materialism and self-interest.

To be sure, this is a revisionary understanding of omnipotence, but it is nevertheless a plausible one. The insight into the power of holiness, peace and self-giving love that it shows is valid. Those who maintain that talk of omnipotence is talk about an all-powerful, timeless and everlasting God need to ask themselves what is gained by such talk.

Summary

What is meant by talk of God's omnipotence will vary depending on whether the word "God" refers (i) to an everlasting spirit or timeless substance or (ii) to either the realist or anti-realist revisionary understanding of language about God set out in Chapters Six and Seven.

1. If God is timeless or everlasting, the most plausible definition of God's omnipotence is the ability of this God to do everything that it is logically possible for God to do. Much will depend on one's definition of God's nature. Descartes' view that God could do anything, including the logically impossible, is fundamentally flawed.

2. A revisionary understanding of omnipotence is possible whereby it is seen as talk about the power of love and holiness. Omnipotence, on this view, does not refer to the power of a creator God, but to the power inherent in each one of us if we would give up living for ourselves and instead devote ourselves to others.

THIRTEEN

Omniscience

I have a friend who, when she was a young girl, was nervous of going to the toilet because she thought that God was watching her. Nietzsche refers to the "indecency" of the Christian God who sees and knows all things – intruding into our privacy.

If omnipotence is one of the most important aspects of the Rubik cube of God, omniscience is certainly another. God, the believer often maintains, knows everything. He is *omnipresent* (present everywhere throughout his creation as well as outside of it) and nothing can be hid from Him. God has numbered every hair on our heads and knows every sparrow that falls. God's knowledge helps to assure the believer that, as Julian of Norwich put it, "All shall be well and all manner of things shall be well." Julian herself could not see how this was the case, but she trusted in God, and this was at least partly because God's knowledge was not in any way limited.

As always, however, once we start to think seriously about what it means to talk of God knowing everything, complexities and difficulties arise, and much depends on the view of God which one adopts. Let us, therefore, look at the possibilities in turn.

The timeless omniscient God

Put simply, the problem is that if God is outside time, how can He know what is happening within time?

Timeless God knows. However, the meaning of the verb "to know" will be different when applied to timeless God than when used of human beings or other animals. Our knowledge is essentially temporal, while God's knowledge is timeless. In fact, as we have seen, it is wrong to apply verbs like "to know" univocally to God. God knows timelessly. To apply the word "know" to God is to use the word analogically. What it means for God to know and what it means for human beings to know will be different. This does not, however, prevent it being true that God knows truths about the temporal universe.

Timeless God, who is literally outside time, sees the past, the present and the future simultaneously. This God, we have previously seen, is like an observer on a mountain looking down on the road of time and seeing all points on that road at once. Time does not pass for God, but all time is present to God. It follows that every event that has ever happened is simultaneously present to God. The age of the dinosaurs, the empire of Alexander the Great, the Civil War in North America, the troubles of the Vietnamese boat people and the end of the world are all, alike, present to timeless God.

Supporters of timeless God will, therefore, argue for a very strong version of omniscience. Timeless God knows everything – past, present and future. To God, of course, there is no past, no present and no future, since all temporal events are simultaneously present to Him. However, He knows at what point on the road of time our lives lie. Such a God knows our future absolutely – in every detail.

This is an attractive view, but it raises a serious problem. If God knows events which are future to us – even though they are not future to Him, because they are timelessly present to Him – in what sense can we be free? If God timelessly knows that my eleven-year-old daughter, Catherine, will marry a man called David on her twenty-seventh birthday, has Catherine (or David!) any choice in the matter!

To put it another way, if God knows our future, is our future wholly determined, and are we like puppets under the control of a puppet master? Parts of the Christian tradition have implied this. The whole idea of *predestination*, which implies that our lives are determined by God, can be seen as opposed to human freedom. Yet, on the other hand, God is meant to have given us human beings the gift of freedom so that we can choose to turn towards Him or away from Him. Love requires us to be free, and if our actions are wholly determined and controlled by God, then we cannot be free.

Anthony Kenny helpfully explains Luther's understanding of predestination: "The human will is like a beast of burden. If God rides it it wills and goes where God wills; if Satan rides it it wills and goes where Satan wills. It must go where its rider bids and it is not free to choose its rider." Kenny says that Luther claims: "Both good and bad men do what they want; what they lack is the ability to change their desires. The human will is not free in the sense that it cannot change itself from a bad will into a good one; it can only passively undergo such a change at the hand of God" (*The God of the Philosophers*, p. 73).

If this is indeed true, then God can timelessly know our future actions and no problem arises, since human beings are not really free. They do not have genuine freedom. However, it is highly questionable whether Luther's view of predestination is right. Human freedom is stronger than he implies. We, as human beings, can make choices and can direct our lives towards or away from God. God does not control us as Luther implies – if He did, then our love would not be free. We would be like puppets on God's strings.

If, therefore, we have genuine freedom and are not controlled by God, are there not real problems with the idea that God knows our future? If timeless God knows our future actions, what sense can be made of the belief that we are free? Boethius, who was a Consul in ancient Rome, addressed this problem. He was falsely accused and put into gaol, and his family were similarly treated. His book, the *Consolation of Philosophy*, was written in prison and was a dialogue between him and his "kindly nurse, Philosophy", in whose company he had lived since his youth. He complained to "the Lady Philosophy" that he had been a just and virtuous man, seeking to govern the Roman State fairly. He referred to Plato's injunction (in the *Republic*) that the ideal state should be governed by philosophers who would be wise enough to be genuinely interested in the good of the state. Boethius was a philosopher and had done all he could to govern the state well, and yet his reward was to have his possessions stripped from him and to be thrown into gaol. The book was an attempt to make sense of his plight.

Boethius says to the Lady Philosophy that God knows everything. God therefore knows the future actions of human beings, and this must mean that men and women are not free. However, the Lady Philosophy replies that this is a mistake. God does, indeed, timelessly know what we shall do in the future, but his knowledge is *not causal*. God timelessly sees our future free actions, but what He sees is the result of our freedom – God does not cause us to act in any particular way.

On this basis, therefore, God can timelessly know all human actions – past, present and future – without taking away human freedom. Our free actions are what God sees, and His seeing does not cause us to act in a certain way. God timelessly knows that my daughter Catherine will marry David in sixteen years' time, but it will be Catherine and David who will decide to get married – God will not cause them to do so.

Believers in timeless God will be realists about the future. They will say, in other words, that statements about the future are either true or they are false. So it is either true or it is false, today, that Catherine will marry David in sixteen years' time. To be sure, we may not know whether this is true, and as Catherine at present does not even know a male named David, it may seem highly unlikely, but that is not the point. Realists maintain a correspondence theory of truth, and in their view a future statement is true if it corresponds to the true state of affairs which is timelessly present to God. A future state of affairs is, therefore, there to be known, and realism about the future is a justifiable position.

The everlasting omniscient God

Timeless God knows the past, the present and the future absolutely, as all time is present to Him. The position is different, however, with the everlasting God, who is in time. To the everlasting God, the future is future and the past is past. There is no problem with such a God knowing the past and the present completely. The difficulties arise with knowledge of the future.

There is no problem in claiming that the everlasting God can know future events which depend on the present situation in the universe. The everlasting God can know today that the sun will rise tomorrow, and He can know the date on which Haley's Comet will return to the Solar System. This information is available to human beings as well, since celestial events behave according to known laws. Can everlasting God, however, know the future free actions of human beings?

There are two basic possibilities, which depend on the way we define human freedom:

1. *Genuine freedom*
Genuine freedom (termed "liberty of indifference" by philosphers) is the freedom to act according to our own choices in

ways that are not wholly determined by our genetic make-up or by our upbringing and background. Human beings do, on this basis, have a measure of genuine freedom which is not determined by their nature. Obviously, this freedom is restricted – I do not have the freedom to fly out of my window or to make myself invisible. Nevertheless, I do have freedom to make moral choices, and these choices are not entirely determined by my nature.

God cannot know the future free actions of human beings, as there is no truth there to be known. We are able to choose what to do with our lives, and God cannot *know* what choices will be made. Of course, God may be able to predict the future free choices of human beings with considerable accuracy, but to say that God knows the future necessarily means that He cannot be mistaken. If, therefore, men and women are free (in the way defined here), God's omniscience cannot extend to knowledge of the future actions of human beings.

On this basis, the everlasting God can still be held to be omniscient. Such a God knows everything that it is logically possible to know. He thus knows all true propositions about the past and the present, but the future is simply not there to be known. It is, therefore, no limitation on God's omniscience to deny Him knowledge of the future actions of human beings, since the future is open and full of many possibilities which will not be determined until human free choices have been made.

The problem with this attractive view is that God's knowledge really is restricted by it. He would not have known in 1900 that the horrors of Auschwitz would take place; He would not have known in the 1950s that Eastern Europe would move away from Communism; He would not know now what the future holds, except to the extent that the future is outside human control. Such limitation on God may be held to be unacceptable.

2. *Freedom to act according to our nature*

If freedom is the freedom to act according to our nature (termed "liberty of spontaneity" by philosophers), then human beings are free to do whatever they wish to do – but what they wish to do is determined by their nature, background and education.

If a person were hypnotised so that he or she felt compelled to act in a certain way, he or she would still be regarded as having freedom to act according to our nature, since he or she would be acting as he or she would want to – even though these wants were determined by the hypnotist. We may have the freedom to act in accordance with our nature, but our nature may be wholly determined. This view of human freedom may therefore be compatible with the view that human actions are controlled and determined by God. We would think that we were free, but we would not have the freedom to choose between alternative courses of action in a way that was not determined by our nature.

If we have this form of freedom – and there is no way, in principle, of proving which type of freedom we have – then the everlasting God could know, in the present, future free actions, since these actions would be wholly determined by our nature.

Most theologians and philosophers want to maintain that we have genuine freedom and, therefore, if they work with a model of God as everlasting they are willing to restrict God's knowledge of the future, so far as this future is affected by the free actions of human beings. Peter Geach has produced a helpful way of looking at God's knowledge of our future free actions. Geach likens God to a Grand Chessmaster. If we were playing chess with a Grand Master, we would be completely free to make any move on the board. There would be no external constraint on us, but there would also be no doubt that we would lose. Geach puts it this way:

God is the supreme Grand Master who has everything under his control. Some of the players are consciously helping his plan, others are trying to hinder it; whatever the finite players do, God's plan will be executed; though various lines of God's play will answer to various moves of the finite players. God cannot be surprised or thwarted or cheated or disappointed. God, like some Grand Master at chess, can carry out his plan even if he has announced it beforehand. "On that square," says the Grand Master, "I will promote my pawn to Queen and deliver checkmate to my adversary," and it is even so.

(*Providence and Evil*, p. 58)

The idea of God as a Grand Master is, in my view, helpful, but not in the way Geach presents it. On his view, the Grand Master can, somehow, predict every move the finite opponents will make, and this interferes with human freedom. Even I, a very weak chess player, could prevent a grand master from "promoting his pawn to Queen and delivering checkmate" if he were to announce this plan in advance.

However, Geach's image of the Grand Master can be adapted. Agreed, a grand chessmaster will beat us. So, it may be held, it is with God. The everlasting God knows all the future possibilities that are open to us, even though He does not know specifically which choices we shall make. However, because God is God and we are mere humans, we cannot frustrate God's long-term purposes and intentions – in other words, we cannot thwart God's plans. So I am maintaining that the everlasting God cannot predict with absolute certainty our every future action. However, He can predict that His eventual purposes will triumph, just as the grand master can predict that he will win the game.

This model can be built upon helpfully. The everlasting God could leave us free to make any choices we wish, within the limitations imposed by our humanity. We can do as we wish, and God may well leave us free to make choices for ourselves about the sort of individuals we shall become. We are free to decide whether we shall become people capable of love and self-sacrifice or whether, instead, we will allow the demands of self to take pride of place and thus become cold and indifferent to others. We can choose – and we must take the consequences of our choices. However, God's wider purposes cannot be thwarted. God can, for example, ensure that we do not drag others down with us. We cannot defeat God but we can nevertheless choose our own paths for ourselves.

Exactly what God's purposes are, we may not know, but the picture remains an attractive one. It emphasises God's personality and does not allow his lack of knowledge about our future free actions to take the world out of His control. God interacts with the world. Thus in the Old Testament, God has to act time after time to bring His chosen people back to obedience to Himself. His ultimate act was the sending of His Son, out of love for men and women, to bring people to see the mistakes they were making in their lives. However, even this act was ambiguous – people were left free to ignore it if they wished, and those who shouted "Hosanna" on Palm Sunday were shouting "Crucify him" six days later. God could do nothing about this without destroying human freedom, and if this freedom were taken away, so would be any possibility of people being brought to love God.

The view of God as everlasting – with His omniscience restricted to knowledge of past and present truths as well as future true statements that are directly due to present events (for instance, future states of the physical universe) – emphasises the personality of God and is easy to understand. God knows all future possibilities. He knew the possibility of Auschwitz and Stalin's death camps, but could not have prevented these without destroying human freedom. He does, the believer maintains, act in the world to ensure that His long-term intentions are brought about. The disadvantage is that God has to act in the universe to ensure that the free actions of men and women do not undermine his purposes, and some may hold that this is too anthropomorphic a view of God.

Believers in an everlasting God will be anti-realists about future statements in so far as these statements refer to the future actions of human beings. They will thus deny that there is any truth to be known until the actions take place.

Revisionary views of omniscience

The two views of omniscience we have looked at so far both involve a God who created the universe and who knows things about the universe. Both timeless and everlasting God know past and present facts. The timeless God knows future facts, whereas the everlasting God's knowledge of the future is more problematic. If, however, we adopt one of the two revisionary views of God already discussed, then there is no God who can know in any conventional sense. What, then, are we going to make of talk of omniscience?

On either Sutherland's realist revisionary view of religion or the anti-realist view, religious language tells us something about the human condition. It shows us something about what it means for human beings to live in the world. Talk of omniscience is talk about our inability to evade the reality against which our lives must be measured. We know ourselves and we cannot escape from our own judgement of ourselves.

In the discussion of Sutherland's views, I quoted a reference he makes to Thomas More. In Robert Bolt's play, *A Man for All Seasons*, More – the Lord Chancellor of England – tells the young and ambitious courtier, Rich, who has come to him seeking advancement at court, that his intended ambitions are mistaken. More advises him he should instead become a teacher. If he is a good teacher, More says, "You will know it, your pupils will know it and God will know it." Sutherland claims that in saying "God will know it," More need not be referring to a CIA – a Celestial Intelligence Agency – which monitors the movements of every human being and which will judge and condemn every word or action that is spoken against the will of the power-figure who controls the universe. Such an understanding is too crude.

Instead, to talk of God's omniscience is to show that the different way of living life that is possible cannot be evaded or avoided. The possibility of the life of holiness and self-giving love is available for us to follow or to reject. We cannot, however, hide our doings in secret, since the actions we take make us the sort of people we become. It is this that will decide whether or not we can overcome the trivialisation that death and old age can easily bring.

Aristotle said that, at first, an individual has the power to choose the path of vice or virtue. However, as our lives continue, so the path we have chosen becomes easier and easier. We become set in our ways, and virtue or vice eventually has power over us. We have made ourselves individuals of a certain type. Our sinful doings, therefore, are not things that we vainly try to hide from an omniscient being. Instead, talk of omniscience reminds us that nothing is hidden, since all our hidden sins determine what sort of people we become. We cannot easily escape their effects, nor can we escape our own knowledge of what we have done. Our sins will find us out.

Summary

The timeless God has all time simultaneously present to Him so that events which, to us, are past, present and future are all alike present to Him.

The everlasting God knows the past and the present. Such a God can know the future only insofar as it is determined by the way things are in the universe now. If, therefore, human beings only have the freedom to act in accordance with their determined nature, then it would be possible for the everlasting God to know the future.

If, however, human beings have genuine freedom to choose between alternatives, then the everlasting God cannot know the future insofar as it could be affected by the free choices of human beings. Such a God could still be held to be omniscient, as He would know all that it is logically possible to know.

If we instead adopt one of the revisionary accounts to explain theological language, then talk about omniscience is a way of showing that we cannot escape the effects of our actions. We become the sort of people our acts make us and, in this sense, all that is hidden will be revealed.

FOURTEEN

God's Action in the World

Can God act? Why even ask the question?

Many religious believers will think that the first question verges on the absurd. After all, is not God omnipotent – can God not do everything? Does God not act when miracles occur? Does not the believer ask God to act in response to prayer? Surely, it may be said, by even raising the question the philosopher shows he has not begun to understand what it is that the believer believes. The second question is answered through these objections to the first – our understanding of what it means to talk about prayer, miracles or the creation is going to depend directly on whether or not God is able to act in the world.

Whether or not God can act and, if He can act, then in what way He can act, are central questions amongst theologians and philosophers. The issues are not as straightforward as many believers assume. There are two basic positions that should be contrasted:

1. *The Theist* is a person who believes in a timeless or an everlasting God who is apart from the universe He has created but who is nevertheless continuously and closely involved with it. Such a God is both transcendent and imminent in the universe. Christianity, Islam and Judaism, as traditionally understood, are all Theistic religions, as they believe in such a God.

2.   *The Deist* is a person who believes in a timeless or an
      everlasting God who is apart from the universe He has
      created and who is not in any way involved with it.
      Deism tends to be a highly rational approach to religious
      belief and, although it is not very influential today,
      attracted considerable support in Britain in the seven-
      teenth and eighteenth centuries. We shall not, in this
      chapter, be considering the Deist position at all.

To start with, we need to separate the different ideas of God
we have so far explored and to take seriously the different
approaches to understanding divine action which their supporters will take.

Timeless action

Assume that a child went to Lourdes and was cured there of
cancer which had been pronounced incurable by the doctors
and which X-rays had shown to have ravaged most of her
body. If the child was cured last week and if the cure was due
to an action by God, does this not mean that God must have
acted last week? If God acted last week, then God would
himself be in time.

Assume that a husband prays today for the release of his
wife, who is the victim of a terrorist hijacking. Three hours
after he has prayed, the husband hears on the news that as a
gesture of "kindness and solidarity with the peace-loving
peoples of the world" his wife, alone of all the hijack victims,
has been released by the hijackers and is safe and well. The
husband gives thanks to God, who has acted in response to his
prayer. If God has acted in response to the husband's prayer,
then surely the action must have followed the request. If the
prayer came before the action by God which secured the release of his wife, does not this mean that God must be in time?

Both the above arguments reject the possibility of *timeless action*. In other words they both maintain that, if God is literally outside time, He cannot act in any way in the universe. If God is to act in a temporal universe, then God himself must be temporal. These arguments have been put forward in various places by many writers, but nowhere is the rejection of timeless action clearer than in a book by Nelson Pike called *God and Timelessness*.

This argument has won very widespread acceptance, and it is amazing how many philosophers and theologians have rejected belief in a timeless God because of it. The argument is, however, badly confused and rests on a basic misunderstanding. This misunderstanding is set out clearly in an article by Stump and Kretzmann (in *The Concept of God* ed. T. V. Morris, Oxford, 1987) in the following way:

1. God brought about an effect in time, therefore it follows that
2. God acted in time to bring about this action.

However, there is no need at all to make this link. Augustine, Aquinas and many other major Christian writers who hold that God is literally timeless maintain that the correct position is:

1. God brought about an effect in time, therefore it follows that
2. Since God is timeless, God must have acted timelessly to bring about this effect.

Timeless action, therefore, is held to be able to bring about effects in time. All time is present simultaneously to the timeless God, who can timelessly decide that certain events should occur at certain times. God could, therefore, timelessly hear the prayer of the husband in the above example at 8.00 a.m., and could timelessly bring about the release of his wife at 11.00 a.m. The fact that the result of God's action occurs in our temporal universe does not necessarily require the action itself to be temporal. God, the cause of the temporal effect, can himself be timeless.

God is omnipotent and this, as we have seen, means that He can do anything that it is logically possible for Him to do. It is not, so it is claimed, logically impossible for a timeless God to act timelessly in order to bring about a temporal effect. Therefore, since God can do anything that is logically possible, God is able to do this.

Critics of timeless action seek to argue that actions must necessarily be in time. After all, all human actions are in time. Any action and its effect take place at a certain time, and the same, it can be argued, applies to God. However, this fails to recognise a basic point in Aquinas' philosophy – that we cannot use univocal language about God. (This was explained on pp. 38–44, where it was made clear that, since timeless God is totally different from us, the language we use to speak about temporal beings within the universe cannot have the same sense when applied to the timeless and spaceless creator of all.)

Aquinas maintained that language about God cannot be univocal – it must be analogical. We can know that language about God is true, but we cannot know what it means for this language to truly be applied to God. It is *true* that God timelessly acts, but we do not know what it *means* for this to be true, since we cannot know what timeless and spaceless God is like in Himself. Of course, this implies that we are agnostic about what timeless action means – we cannot understand it. But how could we hope to do so? The advocate of timeless God takes seriously the radical otherness of God, and is not frightened to admit that we are largely ignorant about God's basic nature.

There is, it is therefore agreed, no problem in saying that timeless God acts timelessly to bring about effects in the universe, even though we may not understand how this is done.

Having said this, however, I suggest that there are questions that can be asked of those who uphold the idea of timeless action that may be more persuasive than those set out above. The above defence of timeless action rests on it not being logically impossible for timeless God to act. I am not sure, however, that this is as obviously right as it may appear.

Wittgenstein asked whether a rose can have teeth. If, in other words, a rose were to have teeth, would it any longer be a rose? To take another example, if someone said that they had a car but that this car, although in perfect condition, had no wheels, no engine, no seats, could not travel along the ground, under the ground or above the ground, was permanently rooted to the same spot and consisted entirely of green leaves, could it then still be a car?

Both these examples are intended to show that there are limits to the way language can be used. Language is, of course, dynamic and the meaning of words can change over time, but at a certain time the meaning of words within our public language is to a large extent fixed.

Now to say that the statement, "God acts timelessly" is logically possible is to maintain that there is no contradiction between "God" (understood here as timeless God) and "action" (understood analogically). A statement such as, "This spinster is male" is logically impossible, since to be a spinster an individual must necessarily be female. If, therefore, I were to say, "Peter Vardy acts timelessly," this would be a logical contradiction, since Peter Vardy is a human being and is, without question, temporal.

It is very difficult indeed to show that "God acts time-

BOGLE ACTS TIMELESSLY
A BOGLE IS A TIMELESS ENTITY
The Puzzle of God
HER
IST
CHE
WE
DON
KNO

lessly" is logically impossible. We know that God, in this context, is timeless. To say, therefore, that a God who is timeless does something timelessly seems entirely reasonable. However, I am not convinced that it is. The problem arises from the content given to terms like "act" and "does". It is very difficult to pin down advocates of a timeless God at this point, since both the subject and predicate of their claim are largely unknowns. Let's take this point slowly.

Take the claim: "God acts timelessly."

1. "God" here refers to timeless and spaceless God. We cannot know what the nature of this God is. We cannot understand what it would be like for timeless, spaceless, metaphysically perfect and utterly simple timeless God to exist. This inevitably follows from the fact that God is so other than us. God is creator, we are creatures. We cannot hope to understand the creator with our limited intellect.

2. "Acts" is here meant in an analogical sense. We can say that the word is not being used univocally. It does not have the same sense as it has when applied within the temporal universe. It is true to say that timeless action is possible, but we do not know what this means.

It will be clear from this that we do not really understand at all what it means to talk *either* of timeless God *or* of timeless action. Because of this, it becomes almost impossible to say that there is a logical contradiction. If we cannot understand *either* the subject *or* the predicate of a sentence, how can we possibly claim that there is any contradiction? Aquinas' position appears foolproof.

I do not think there is any certain way of showing that the notion of timeless action is incoherent or logically impossible, but I do believe that the extent of the agnosticism implied by the claim needs to be recognised. When we use the word "action" it does not just have temporal overtones – everything about the word involves time. Actions are carried out by persons, and persons are temporal. Is it possible, then, to take away all the temporal elements and then to leave any significant content to either timeless action or timeless personality?

Take a parallel case. Let's ask the question, "Can God have teeth?" On the face of it the question is absurd. If God is timeless and spaceless, utterly simple and without body or parts, He cannot possibly have teeth. Having teeth would flatly contradict God's spacelessness. However, the same could be said about timeless action. We could say, echoing Aquinas' position, that the word "teeth" cannot be used univocally when applied to God. Clearly, God cannot have teeth as we have teeth, but perhaps God could have teeth analogically or metaphorically. If, however, God has no body of any sort and is utterly timeless, it could be argued that even analogical talk of teeth verges on the absurd. Better to say that God has no teeth than to qualify "teeth" so abstrusely that the word has no remaining meaningful content.

The same might be said of timeless action. If we cannot here understand the word "action" in any of the ways in which it is usually understood, it may be better to say that God cannot act. On this basis it might be held not that talk of timeless action is logically impossible but that it is highly misleading and verges on the incoherent. Better not to use the term rather than to retreat behind mystery and agnosticism to such an extent that no content remains to the word "act".

Before we leave this topic we should consider the difficulties of one particular timeless act. Timeless God is held to have created the universe. Aquinas, interestingly, did not think that this could be proved philosophically and considered that creation was a revealed truth. However, the matter is more problematic than that.

Augustine considered the question, "What did God do before the creation of the universe?" and came to the conclusion that the question was absurd. Time came into existence with the creation (if by this is understood not just the creation of the material universe but also that of celestial beings such as angels), and before there was time there was no time. God existed timelessly, and for timeless God time does not pass. To ask about events before time came into existence is, therefore, nonsensical. This seems reasonable.

However, let us try an exercise in imagination, albeit a very difficult one, as it is an attempt to imagine the unimaginable. Imagine that the creation has not yet taken place. God timelessly exists. There is no matter, no celestial beings, no time – nothing other than timeless God, for whom time does not pass. So we have timeless God, existing without any time frame at all, and nothing beyond Him.

However, if there is no time frame at all, how can the universe come into existence? If the creation is to take place, the universe must begin to exist. God must, timelessly, do the equivalent of saying, "Let there be light" (Genesis 1:3). There is, however, no moment at which this can be said – even timelessly. *Either* the universe must always have existed (in which case, although God may sustain it and keep it in existence, He cannot have created it – a position taken by Schleiermacher) *or* it can never exist. Unless there is some time frame in God himself, unless God is essentially temporal, there can be no time at which the decision is made that the universe must come into existence.

It will not do, on this point, to claim that the creation is a doctrine revealed by God. If God is literally timeless, then it would seem that He *cannot*, logically, have created the universe from nothing. He could, certainly, have sustained a universe which had always existed. We might support this idea if we believe, for instance, in a universe that keeps expanding and contracting, so that after a certain point our present universe will collapse in on itself, only to be followed by another "Big Bang" which will start a new cycle. However, God could not have created this universe in the absence of a time frame.

In the end, the possibility of timeless action remains open. Its advocates can rest on the utter otherness of God, and there seems no conclusive way to disprove their position, even if the idea of timeless creation from nothing seems to suffer from grave philosophic difficulties.

Action by an everlasting God

If God is an everlasting spirit, then action by such a God presents few problems. Indeed, the attractiveness of this view of God rests partly on the relative ease with which we can make sense of God's action. The everlasting God is in time and is able to act in time. God is aware of prayers uttered at time $T1$ and answers them at time $T2$. The future is future to this God, just as the past is past.

We cannot, of course, understand what it would be for God to be an everlasting spirit who is trinitarian (three Persons in one and one Person in three), but such a God can certainly be easily thought of in personal terms. Action is relative to persons, and since the everlasting God is essentially personal, His action is relatively free from philosophic difficulties.

There are questions that need to be asked about when and where God acts in the world, but these are common to both the timeless and the everlasting views of God, and we shall return to them when we discuss prayer and miracles. In particular, a God who is able to act in the world but who does not do so when faced with the tremendous suffering at Auschwitz or in the Armenian earthquake may be held to be a God who is not worth worshipping.

What it means to talk of God's action in the revisionist views of Christianity

In either the realist or the anti-realist revisionary views of Christianity, there is no creator God who is apart from the universe and who interacts with it. On the face of it, therefore, there is no content to talk of God's action. However, this is too simplistic.

Saint Theresa of Avila is said to have written the following lines:

> *Christ has no body now on earth but yours,*
> *No hands but yours, no feet but yours,*
> *Yours are the only eyes through which He is to look*
> *with compassion on the world,*
> *Yours are the feet with which He is to go about doing good,*
> *And yours the hands with which He is to bless us now.*

The picture which St Theresa presents here (different pictures are presented elsewhere in her writings) is not of a creator God who is continuously active in the world: she says God has no other hands but ours, no other feet but ours. It is we, therefore, who must do the acting on behalf of God. It is we who must act for God and show compassion to the world. It is we who must go out among the poor and the weak to show them God's compassion, and the blessing with which we bless others must be the blessing of our love and care.

To talk of God's action, therefore, is to talk of our action. God is acting wherever in the world we find compassion, wherever we find love, wherever the poor are provided for, wherever those in prison are visited, wherever the sick are cared for and the weak are supported and helped.

We do not need, however, to think in terms of a timeless or everlasting God who in some unknowable way acts through people. Rather, acts of compassion and love *are* God's actions – that is what we call acts of compassion and love. This is a powerful and attractive picture. God's actions are seen wherever in the world the power of love is at work.

However, we do have to recognise that this *is* a revisionary view. Saint Theresa does not actually want to go as far as the revisionists want to go. She wants to show that we cannot rely on God to act, and that we must act on behalf of Him. She is not suggesting that God *cannot* or *does not* act. For her, as for mainstream Christianity, God certainly can act directly in the world without human agency – it is just that believers must not rely on this intervention. She would also want to say that God Himself does truly act through people – she would not want to imply that what we call God's actions are really just the acts of individuals behaving in a certain way.

Summary

Timeless action cannot be shown to be impossible, even though advocates of this view would accept that we cannot know what it would mean for timeless God to act. There are, however, problems in saying that timeless God created the universe from nothing.

The everlasting God can certainly act in the world, and there are no philosophic problems with this – other than those difficulties which are common to all forms of divine action. We shall examine these in the next two chapters.

On the anti-realist view, to talk of God's action is to talk of those actions of love, compassion and concern for others done by human beings.

FIFTEEN

Petitionary Prayer

Although there are many different types of prayer, the main problems are associated with two specific types: *petitionary prayer* (which involves asking God for things – asking for help or for guidance or for changes in some state of affairs) and *praying for forgiveness*. The reason why these forms of prayer are the most interesting for philosophic analysis is that there are such diverse interpretations as to what is happening during such prayers. In this chapter we shall look at the first of these and then move on to prayer for forgiveness in the next chapter.

Our understanding of petitionary prayer is going to be directly affected by the type of God in which we believe. There are two broad alternatives:

1. God is a reality within the form of life of the believing community – this is the anti-realist view. Language about God is a way of calling people to a different way of living their lives, but does not refer to a being or spirit who created the world – this is the realist view put forward by Sutherland. Both these views deny that the word "God" refers to a being who created the universe and who interacts with it.

2. God is timeless substance or an everlasting spirit. In either of these cases we are, as we have seen, dealing with a creator God who is apart from the universe He has

created, but who sustains it and is omnipresent within it.

In both views, prayer is valuable and important – a "worthwhile exercise". In the second of the above views, the believer is claiming that God exists and is capable of acting within the world. In the first view, although language about God is vitally important and prayer is central to the believers' lives, they do not communicate with some being who created and sustains the universe. We are considering these different views in this order, because the understanding of prayer adopted by the revisionists is also likely to be accepted by those who believe there is a creator God (although the latter will want to go a good deal further). It makes sense, therefore, to explore the common ground first.

We saw in Chapter Fourteen that various views are possible about what it means for God to act. In our discussion in this chapter we shall assume that if God is timeless substance, then this God can act timelessly to bring about temporal effects in the world. As we have seen, this position is not universally accepted. If timeless God cannot act, then prayer to such a God will have to be interpreted in terms similar to those used by the revisionists. However, in this chapter we shall assume that timeless God can act.

We have to separate two different understandings of petitionary prayer, based on the two definitions of God outlined in 1. and 2. above:

1.   Petitionary prayer the prime purpose of which is to seek changes in the believer.

2.   Petitionary prayer the prime purpose (although not necessarily the sole purpose) of which is to ask God, who created and sustains the world, to act in response to the prayer.

It must be emphasised that believers in God as the creator who sustains the world may well see petitionary prayer as calling God to act, but may also see the prayer as having an effect on the individual. However, 1., if coupled with one of the revisionist understandings of talk about God, does rule out 2., since there is then no God to act as God is traditionally conceived as acting.

We will consider these two different understandings in turn.

Petitionary prayer the prime purpose of which is to seek changes in the believer

If the word "God" does not refer to a creator God who acts in the world, an account of petitionary prayer is needed which does not involve asking a creator God to act.

The very idea of prayer as asking an agent called God to act can be seen as fundamentally flawed. In his book, *The Concept of Prayer*, D. Z. Phillips has produced an excellent account of prayer which, he claims, avoids the problem of prayer becoming something like superstition. In particular, his account does not see petitionary prayer as asking a creator God to act in the world. Phillips' approach – which draws heavily on the work of Wittgenstein – has great strength and, if a believer reads the book, he or she may well be convinced of the account that is given. This happens with many of my students, who find Phillips totally convincing – until they realise that he is one of the leading anti-realists about truth claims in connection with God. Many of them cannot agree with such a position. However, the fact that his account is convincing to believers with varied ideas of God, at least on first reading, is a testimony to its effectiveness.

Phillips maintains that prayer does not change God; rather, it changes the person uttering the prayer. He contrasts talking to God and talking to a human person and claims that there are both similarities and differences. His account takes petitionary prayer seriously, without involving the idea of a timeless or everlasting God who acts in some mysterious way in the world. Here is a summary of Phillips' account of prayer:

1.   Prayer to God requires genuine devotion. We can decide whether prayer is genuine by looking at the role it has in an individual's life.

2.   Prayer involves coming to self-knowledge, meditation on one's wants and "bringing them before God". In prayer, the believer is recognising his or her wants before the existing reality that is God. (We must remember that for Phillips God certainly exists – but not as a creator who is apart from the universe that He has created. God exists as a reality within the form of life of the believing community. To say that Phillips does not believe in God is to seriously misunderstand the anti-realist position.)

3.   Prayer is a way of finding meaning and hope in life. For example, the believer who prays for help to pass an examination does not really do so in the hope that God will improve his or her performance beyond the level he or she deserves; rather, by prayer he or she is enabled to live with success or failure, and thus overcome domination by externals. A boxer may cross himself before a fight or a mother may put flowers in front of the statue of the Virgin Mary; Phillips claims that the boxer is not asking for help to win the fight, nor is the mother asking that her child should get better. Instead their prayer is that they should be able to live with whatever the future holds, whether this is victory or defeat, death or life.

4.   Wittgenstein gives an example of the tribe that prays for rain every year at the time when it is due to rain in any case. It might be claimed that this is similar to the Church of England's Rogation and Harvest Thanksgiving services. The Rogation service takes place in the spring and asks for God's blessing on the crops, whilst at the Harvest Thanksgiving (one of the very best attended of the Church of England's services in the year) believers give thanks for the harvest. However bad or good the harvest, believers still give thanks.

Phillips claims that Wittgenstein's example of the tribe praying for rain is intended to show that there is no objective point to the ritual dance – the prayer takes place when the rain is due in any case. Instead there is a subjective point. The prayer is expressive. The believer is expressing feelings of dependence and is recognising his or her part in the totality of the earth. The believer is definitely *not* asking for God to intervene in some way to change the weather.

When the Catholic goes to mass, when the Muslim prays five times a day, when the Jew goes to the synagogue, he or she is recognising his or her finitude and getting away from the world so as to reorder his or her priorities.

5.   The pious form of petitionary prayer is, "Thy will be done." This is the key to all such prayer. Petitionary prayer is answered, no matter what happens. The point of such prayer does not lie in any eventual outcome but in the effect that such prayer has on the individual(s) making the prayer. It is a way of finding meaning and hope in life, whatever happens.

6.   Prayer is not a substitute for effort. One cannot pray and then sit back in the hope that God will do the necessary work. Instead, prayer is a means of accepting whatever will be the case. *It is a ritual the point of which lies in itself.* When a Christian, Muslim or Jew goes to church, mosque or syna-

gogue, Phillips might say, he or she goes apart from the world, reorders his or her thoughts and priorities and possibly his or her future actions in certain ways and comes out feeling renewed. The believer must act in the world and bring about God's purposes, and it is through petitionary prayer that the believer is helped to recognise what needs to be done.

7. Petitionary prayer thus brings about a change in the believer. Through it he or she comes to recognise that his or her desires are not those of God. The believer comes to see his or her life and actions in a new way.

In this approach, if a father is praying for his five-year-old child who is dying in terrible pain from throat cancer, what he is doing, if he is not superstitious, is simply meditating in such a way that he can bring himself to face whatever the outcome of the disease may be. Specifically, he is *not* praying for a miracle to cure his child. Anyone who thinks that this is what he is doing is, in Phillips' view, highly superstitious.

In this view petitionary prayer changes the person who prays. God may not be an everlasting spirit or timeless substance, but it is true that God exists within the form of life of the believing community. This view has great strengths:

1. It takes seriously the connection between prayer and the rest of life. Someone who prays in a moment of crisis – for instance, when about to drown at sea – is not praying on this view. (On the other hand, is this position valid? Can a prayer in a moment of crisis not be a genuine prayer, even if one's whole life is not dedicated to God? Are not deathbed repentances possible? In Tolstoy's *The Death of Ivan Illyich*, it is only at the point of death that Ivan realises that his life has been meaningless. Would prayer in such circumstances not be valid?)

2. Phillips' account of prayer is particularly strongly related to a religious way of life – as, of course, it has to be, as it finds meaning for language about God within this framework.

3. The idea of men's and women's total dependence on God is taken seriously. We cannot just ask for things when we need them. God is not to be seen as a cosmic slot machine of which we make requests and from which we expect actions in return. Prayer is part of the way of life of the believing community.

4. Phillips' account recognises that petitionary prayer is always valid and that its validity does not depend on it being "answered" or "unanswered". Prayer helps the believer to recognise his or her desires before God and to find meaning and hope, whatever happens. There is more to prayer than getting something out of God.

5. "Thy will be done" is recognised as the central part of Christian prayer. This is in accordance both with the Lord's prayer ("Thy will be done in heaven and on earth") and with Jesus' prayer in Gethsemene ("Nevertheless, not my will but thine be done").

6. Although Phillips does not stress the effect of prayer on the community, his model of petitionary prayer could easily be extended to take this into account. By expressing prayer in a religious service, the community of believers may be helped to focus their wills and their actions on the needs expressed by the prayer. In praying for relief for those suffering in the third world, the members of the community are reminded of their own responsibilities to the third world and are thereby moved to take necessary action. Similarly, in praying for the ecumenical movement, members of the believing community are

brought to recognise their own responsibility to seek understanding and to build bridges between different denominations.

Strong though this account is, there are nevertheless real problems as well as advantages:

1. Wittgenstein said that philosophy should leave everything as it is. If the non-believer would understand religious language, he or she should seek to understand the role this language plays in the believer's life. Phillips is meant to be a follower of Wittgenstein, yet in this he is unfaithful to his master. His approach is partly prescriptive – it lays down what the believer is or should be doing, not what the believer thinks is happening. So in this sense it is right to label him a revisionist. He is revising believers' understanding of prayer, not seeking to understand what they are doing. He may, of course, be right to do this – but it is a prescriptive and revisionary exercise.

2. Most believers *do* think they are talking to a God who created the universe and who still interacts with it. To them prayer is not just therapy or "getting something off your chest". Phillips says that people who actually do think they are asking God to act in the world are very superstitious. On this basis, Jesus himself was highly superstitious.

3. Phillips wants to compartmentalise our lives. Prayer may be held to be not just something that happens within the religious form of life and not outside it. It may be held that we are part of a wider reality and that even those who are not normally religious can nevertheless pray. It has been said that there were no atheists in the trenches in the First World War, in that almost every person there, in their fear and loneliness,

would have prayed – yet not many would have regarded themselves as being religious in normal life.

4. Prayer may be part of a two-way relationship between the creator God and the individual and in the context of such an I/Thou relationship, requests for God to act *are* made.

Prayer on this view is a form of meditative therapy and certainly has meaning, purpose and value. When Jesus was praying in Gethsemene he was – on this view – facing up to the reality of what was likely to happen to him the following day. He was an intelligent man. He could not have rejected the pious church leaders, so sure of their own holiness, who controlled the synagogue without getting into very real trouble.

Jesus prayed and in praying faced up to the imminence of his death and, because of his prayer, found the strength within himself to go through with it.

The disadvantages of this approach do, however, need to be taken seriously and whilst the believer in timeless or an everlasting God may agree that there is much to commend in Phillips' account, they will also maintain that there is more to petitionary prayer than seeking changes in the believer.

Petitionary Prayer to timeless or an everlasting God

On this view, God is an agent who can act in the world (we are assuming for the purpose of this discussion that timeless God can act – see Ch. 14). Petitionary prayer is, at least partly, about asking God to intervene. The question is, in what way is the process meant to work?

Christianity has traditionally maintained that it is permissible to pray for things to happen and that, indeed, things sometimes do happen as a result of prayer. If this is so, prayer must be capable of influencing the activity of God.

Aquinas maintained that God timelessly knows what all believers will pray and has timelessly taken these prayers into account as part of the total causal sequence. God's timeless knowledge of the prayers of believers is one of the factors that God takes into account in deciding whether to act in the world.

Aquinas distinguishes between God as *Primary Cause* and as *Secondary Cause*. God is primary cause of everything since God sustains the universe and everything in it at all times. Without God, nothing would exist. God is, therefore, the primary cause of both Mother Teresa of Calcutta and also of Hitler since both are kept in existence by his sustaining power.

When human beings act, they are only able to do so because God keeps them in existence and gives them the power to act. Normally it is human beings who act as secondary causes, but they are sustained by God who is primary cause. However it is possible for God to act directly in the universe without this action being mediated through the action of human beings. In other words, God is quite capable of acting directly in the universe in response to petitionary prayer.

"Everything God wills comes about" says Aquinas (S.T. 1a, 19, 8). God's action can either be direct, a primary action, or action through human beings under the principle of *Double Agency*. This claims that when individuals or groups of people act, they may in fact be acting on behalf of God so there can be a double agency – the agency (or action) of both the individual or group and of God. Both agents are present in the one action. God can, therefore, be seen as acting through people.

A dramatic example of this was when the prophet Jeremiah told the Israelites that God was going to send them into exile, and that God was going to use the Babylonians as the agent to punish them for their disobedience. The Babylonians would defeat them in war and Jerusalem would be torn down. Although the obvious agent was the Babylonian army, Jeremiah says that God is acting through them. God's hand, therefore, is seen in history and in individual human actions.

Aquinas had some difficulty accounting for unanswered prayer and does not really explain why some prayers are answered whilst others are not. He may well have felt that no further explanation was necessary beyond an assertion of God's will. Aquinas was, as we have seen, happy to work with a model of God which lay beyond human understanding. Although we can use language about God which is true, we do not know what it means for this language to be true when applied to God (p. 43). We should not, therefore, be surprised by any reluctance to speculate about God's motives and intentions. Even in the Beatific Vision which faithful believers will, on Aquinas' view, experience at the end of time and in which they will be given all knowledge, knowledge of God's motives and intentions is specifically excluded.

In contrast to the Thomist timeless God, Vincent Brummer, in his book *What are we doing when we pray?*, provides an account of petitionary prayer which is based on the everlasting God model. Crucial to Brummer's understanding of prayer is the two-way relationship between God and the believer. He sees the I/Thou relationship, as Martin Buber puts it, as the cornerstone of any understanding of prayer. This idea of a personal relationship between an individual and God has been a key element in Christian understanding although it may be held to be more difficult to conceive of God's immutable, unknowable, timeless substance than of God as an everlasting spirit.

Brummer claims that petitionary prayer does involve asking God to act. Brummer says that without our prayers, God could bring about what we need but he could not give us anything, since for something to be a gift it must be recognised as such. To the non-believer, everything that occurs happens as a result of chance. The rain falls, beneficial coincidences occur, people recover from operations – all these are seen as the mere working of the natural order. However, the believer, who looks upon the whole of his or her life as a relationship with God, will see these things as gifts. Brummer quotes Lucas (*Theology and Grace*), who says:

> God sends the rain to the just and the unjust; but to the just who has asked for it, it comes as a token of God's goodness, whereas to the unjust who never says "Please" and never says "Thank you", it is a mere climatic condition, without significance and without being an occasion for gratitude; and the unjust's life is poorer thereby.

no

On this basis, the Church of England's Rogation and Harvest Thanksgiving services need not just be rituals the point of which lies in themselves (as the revisionists would suggest). Instead they can be seen as expressing a realist truth claim – that the whole universe actually is dependent on the creator God as the primary cause, and that all human beings ultimately depend on this God. Only by seeing the world in this way do we see the world correctly. These services help to remind believers of their utter dependence on God.

So far, however, Brummer's account could also be adopted by the revisionists, as they could say that the truth expressed is an anti-realist claim. It is a claim that is true for the believer, but not for the non-believer. All Brummer is doing, the revisionists might say, is to affirm that prayer is intended to alter the believer's perspective on the world. They, also, would be happy to talk of dependence – even though, in their view, there is no creator God upon whom we are dependent. Brummer claims that the creator God *does* act in answer to prayer, although in order to see God's action one must have the appropriate outlook. In his book (pp. 70–71) he distinguishes two positions which correspond to the realist and anti-realist attitudes which we have previously discussed, although he does not make use of these terms. The two positions are as follows:

1. A difference of interpretation where there is no one correct view – as in the case of Wittgenstein's sketch (which has since become famous), the subject of which could either be seen as a duck or as a rabbit. This is akin to the anti-realist view. On this basis, some events would be seen as acts of God by the believer, whilst to the non-believer they would be mere coincidences. Both positions would be equally valid and equally true within their respective forms of life.

2. A difference of interpretation where one view is right and another is wrong. This is the realist view. The believer is claiming that it is true that God has acted in response to prayer, and that this truth is based on a correspondence between the statement, "God has acted" and the action by an incorporeal, divine agent.

Brummer effectively maintains (without using this language) that the believer is making a *realist* claim about God's action – in other words he is saying that the believer's claims are true because they correspond to the way the world is. However, he does not explain how this claim could be justified. He also does not sufficiently discuss the problems connected with the view that petitionary prayer does involve asking an agent called God to intervene. These problems include the following:

1. God is held to be omnipotent, omniscient and wholly good. However, if God knows everything and is wholly

good, why should a believer have to pray? If God knows all the needs of the believer and loves him or her, surely He will bring about everything that is needed without being asked. As Helen Oppenheimer puts it: "What is hard to believe in is a God who is supposed to withhold his favour from some apparently worthy person or cause for whom no-one has happened to pray."

2. Unanswered prayer is a real problem. If God answers some prayers but then does not respond to a father whose child is starving, what is the believer to say? We might, perhaps, claim that it was for the good of the father's soul that the child should starve to death. However, if we think of the suffering of the children who were thrown alive into mass graves at Auschwitz or of those who were killed in the Armenian earthquake, this seems – at the very least – a questionable position.

3. Jesus told his followers that whatever they asked in his name they would receive, and that faith could move mountains. These words do not fit in easily with the deafening silence that appears to follow many petitionary prayers. If we think of the numbers of prayers for peace in Northern Ireland, or for relief for the starving in the third world, or for cures for children dying of terrible diseases, explanations are not easy.

4. If petitionary prayer genuinely does make a difference, it should be possible to produce statistical evidence that believers who pray are more likely to survive serious illnesses than people who do not pray; that the starvation rates amongst believers are lower than amongst non-believers; that earthquakes and other natural disasters affect the faithful less than the unfaithful. There is, however, no such evidence. Indeed, it was God's chosen people, the Jews – to whom, the

Bible says, God made a commitment – who were extermi-
nated by the Nazis. Can we really say that, in the same way as
God used the Babylonians in the Old Testament, he also used
the Nazis to punish the Jews for their sins? Surely any such
suggestion is offensive and would point to a morally debased
view of God.

I have to say that I know of no intellectually satisfactory
way to answer these points *if* a creator God is affirmed.
Outsiders to the belief systems which affirm that God acts in
the world are unlikely to find answers to these problems
which they would consider philosophically satisfying. Many
believers do not feel the need for such answers and are content
to retreat behind mystery. As the prophet says: "The right-
eous shall live by his faith" (Habbakuk 2:4) – in other words,
the believer must live in trust and reliance on God. Even
though he or she may recognise the problems, these will not
affect his or her belief in or relationship with God.

The magnificent chapters 38 to 40 of the book of Job affirm
this position. When Job seeks to understand his plight, God
refuses to give any answer and says, effectively, that Job
cannot understand His ways. The philosophic difficulties,
however, are part of the reason why some believers increasingly see petitionary prayer as solely a matter of bringing
about changes in the believer and in the community of which
he or she is a part.

Summary

The understanding one has of petitionary prayer will largely
depend on the model of God with which one is operating. In
all views of God, petitionary prayer will be seen as meditative, as having therapeutic value and as bringing about
changes in the believer and in members of his or her commu-

nity. In both the realist and the anti-realist revisionary accounts of language about God (in other words, where God is a reality within the form of life of the believing community or where talk about God is talk about a possible way of living life), this will be all that petitionary prayer involves.

If God is timeless substance or an everlasting spirit, then prayer can form part of a two-way, I/Thou relationship with God in which the believer makes requests which God may or may not answer. Which prayers are answered and which are not is put down to God's discretion, and there is no human way of understanding the motives and intentions that lie behind God's free decisions in this area.

There are considerable philosophic difficulties with the idea of a God who can act in the world and who chooses to do so in such a selective fashion – ignoring requests which we, as human beings, would not fail to respond to if we had the power to do so. Some believers will be happy to ignore this, trusting in God's wisdom, which is held to surpass anything that human beings can understand.

SIXTEEN

Praying for Forgiveness

Every Christian, Muslim or Jew who takes part in any form of worship prays for forgiveness. Almost without exception services include confessions of sin. In some churches, there are not only *general confessions* (confessions of sin made by the whole congregation using a set form of words) but also *personal confessions* in which an individual either goes to a priest to confess his or her sins and to be absolved from them, or else confesses his or her sins to the community of which he or she forms a part. A typical general confession is that used by the Church of England in its *Alternative Services Book 1980*:

> *Almighty God, our heavenly Father,*
> *We have sinned against you and against our fellow men,*
> *in thought and word and deed,*
> *through negligence, through weakness,*
> *through our own deliberate fault.*
> *We are truly sorry*
> *and repent of all our sins.*
> *For the sake of your Son Jesus Christ, who died for us,*
> *forgive us all that is past;*
> *and grant that we may serve you in newness of life*
> *to the glory of your name. Amen.*

The question we need to ask is what the believer thinks is happening when he or she prays for forgiveness. One question that obviously arises here is what is meant by sin. There can be many different approaches. Sin may be seen as (i) breaking rules, such as the ten commandments; (ii) acting against the law of love; (iii) turning away from God or (iv) ceasing to live up to our true human nature. We shall not be discussing the different approaches to sin because, whatever view is taken, praying for forgiveness involves seeking to deal with the situation that the believer's sins have created. Certainly, praying for forgiveness involves repentance, and this must be genuine. Sorrow for sins committed is an essential part of any genuine prayer for forgiveness.

The different possibilities can well be illustrated by a series of diagrams involving the following four possible parties:

The individual

It is true that in some churches prayers for forgiveness do not ask for forgiveness of an individual but rather for forgiveness of a group of people. You will notice that the prayer above says, "We have sinned against you and our fellow men." However, any community is made up of individuals. It is not the community that is guilty so much as all those who make up the community. They share, in different ways, in the guilt. Sin is an individual business, although it is true that some sins can result from sharing in evil structures – for instance, it might be held that the affluent, materialistic and selfish lifestyle of the western world is sinful because millions are starving in the third world. However, this corporate sin cannot remove responsibility from each of us, as individuals, for our part in that sin. This point is made by Rudyard Kipling's poem *Tomlinson*, about a man of that name who dies and comes before St Peter at Heaven's entrance gate. Saint Peter says:

*"Stand up, stand up now, Tomlinson, and answer loud and
   high*
*The good that ye did for the sake of men or ever ye came to
   die –*
*The good that ye did for the sake of men on little earth so
   lone!"*
*And the naked soul of Tomlinson grew white as a
   rain-washed bone.*
*"Oh, I have a friend on earth," he said, "that was my priest
   and guide,*
And well would he answer all for me if he were at my side."
"For that ye strove in neighbour-love it shall be written fair,
*But now ye wait at Heaven's Gate and not in Berkeley
   Square:*
*Though we called your friend from his bed this night, he
   could not speak for you,*
*For the race is run by one and one and never by two and
   two."*
*Then Tomlinson looked up and down, and little gain was
   there,*
*For the naked stars grinned overhead, and he saw that his
   soul was bare . . .*

Christianity, Islam and Judaism have all affirmed in their
different ways that "the race is run by one and one and never
by two and two." Further on in the poem Tomlinson comes
face to face with the Devil, and the same point is made again:
"For the sin ye do by two by two, ye must pay for one by
one." In other words, we must take responsibility for our
own actions. We cannot hide behind membership of a community in order to disclaim individual responsibility.

Praying for forgiveness is something that each individual
must do – whether together with or apart from others.
Individuality cannot be subsumed under any broader

category. It is we as individuals who act, we who live our lives and we who must take the consequences of the choices we make.

The priest

In some churches priests are not particularly important theologically – at least in terms of any hierarchial status. They are not any different from the ordinary members of the congregation, even though they may be leaders of their community. This might apply, for instance, in the Baptist, Methodist, Pentecostal or Reformed churches. In the Catholic, Orthodox and Anglican Churches on the other hand, the priest is a theologically pivotal figure – able to pronounce forgiveness of sins in a way that no layman can do. The different models below, therefore, sometimes incorporate the priest and sometimes do not.

The community

The Catholic Church, in particular, stresses the importance of community. Indeed "community" has become a key phrase amongst Catholics since the Second Vatican Council, and it is difficult to find a Catholic pronouncement that does not feature the word. To be a Catholic is, to a very real extent, to belong to the Catholic community. All churches have some sense of community, and in praying for forgiveness one of the things the believer may be doing is becoming reconciled to his or her community, because he of she has sinned against it.

God

We need two views of God in order to take account of the two main possibilities:

The creator God: This is the timeless or everlasting God who is an agent who created the universe. In prayer for forgiveness this God may well be involved and can respond to that prayer. It makes sense to talk of a two-way relationship with this God.

God: This is the anti-realist view of God. God is not in any sense an agent; God did not create the universe. God does, indeed, exist and is a reality within the form of life of the believing community. God may well be essential as a focus for the believers' prayers, but God does not and cannot respond, as this God is not in any sense personal.

With these basic categories established, we can now move on to look at the different interpretations of what it means to pray for forgiveness.

Model 1

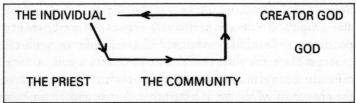

John prays for forgiveness and meditates about his life. He thinks about how he has failed to follow the path of love, how he has been unkind to his parents, how he has lied to his sister and how he has been selfish. He thinks about the hurt he has caused and is genuinely sorry. He resolves to try very hard to mend his ways and to be the kind and loving person he would really like to be in the future. Having recognised his sins, he goes on his way refreshed – he knows where he is and is resolved to do better in the future.

On this model, praying for forgiveness involves John in coming to self-knowledge. When he prays, he measures his life against his ideal and recognises his failings. He sees himself as he really is and resolves to become a better person. He is thus able to live with himself.

Sutherland quotes the example of the man who, in Dostoyevsky's *The Brothers Karamazov*, confesses to a priest the murder he committed fifteen years previously. Because of the confession, the man is able to come to terms with what he has done and to find the strength to continue his life, freed from the chains of his past sin. However, no priest is necessary in order for this to be possible – although some people may find it psychologically helpful to confess out loud to someone else. In this view, the sole purpose of prayer for forgiveness is a psychological and meditative one. Confession is a matter of coming to human wholeness and of finding that one can cope with one's failures and not be handicapped by a legacy of guilt from the past.

Such a view might well be adopted by those, such as Stewart Sutherland, who take a realist approach to language about God and who affirm that talk about God is talk about a possible way in which the individual can live his or her life.

Anne prays for forgiveness and meditates upon her life, measuring it against the reality of God which is affirmed by the church of which she is a member. She thinks about how she has failed to follow the path of love, how she has fiddled her expense claim at the office, how she was unpleasant to her friend Ruth when she was unhappy, how she always puts herself first. Anne recognises her mistakes and how she has failed to be a proper member of her community. She resolves to act differently, to repay the fiddled expenses and to telephone Ruth and go to see her. She is determined that, in future, she really will live up to the values in which she and her community believe.

Model 2

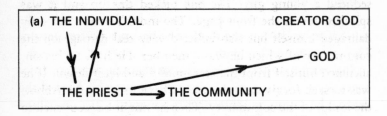

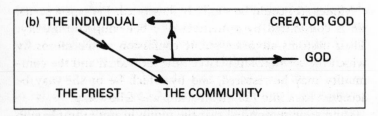

In Model 2(a), Anne will go to the priest to tell him about her sins. In Model 2(b) she will not feel that this is necessary.

In both these models God is involved, but it is the anti-realist God – not the creator God of traditional Christianity (if you are not clear about this, refer to the definitions at the beginning of this chapter). In Models 2(a) and 2(b) praying for forgiveness has the same psychological and therapeutic effects as set out in Model 1, but in addition Anne is reconciled to the community of which she is a part. In Model 2(a) this happens through the priest who, as the leader of the community, is able to grant reconciliation, whereas in Model 2(b) no priest is necessary, and the reconciliation between the individual and the community is direct.

The idea of someone being reconciled to the community to which he or she belongs may seem strange to some readers. An example may help to explain this. I once gave a talk to some Benedictine monks on the philosophic problems involved in prayer, and the following was one of the examples which I used. Imagine that one of the monks had seduced a young girl. *The Sun* picked this up and it was splashed across the front page. The monk's action not only damaged himself but also inflicted very real damage on the community of which he was a member. He had, by his sin, alienated himself from the community and let it down. If he was to seek forgiveness, he would have to go to the Abbot, the leader of the community. Then he might be reconciled to the members of the brotherhood.

Model 2(b) could be similarly illustrated. Perhaps a sexual sin is committed by a member of a believing community. Their customs advocate public confession as the means by which the relationship between the individual and the community may be restored, and by which he or she may be accepted back into full membership and fellowship.

It must be recognised that the monk in my example who has sinned and who is reconciled back to the community may well feel comforted and forgiven, but questions do need to be asked about the girl who was seduced and who may have no community to support her. Sometimes there can be too great a concentration on the effects of sin on the sinner and not enough on the possibly graver effects of sin on the person who was sinned against. However, this is a wider issue which can be relevant to all models of praying for forgiveness.

Model 3

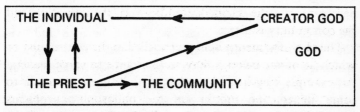

Andrew knows that he has sinned against the God who

created him and to whom he owes total loyalty. He knows that he has been selfish. Instead of trying to come closer to God and to show others the love of God, he has been indifferent and hard, concentrating solely on his business and on increasing profits. He knows that he is like the people in the Bible whom Jesus criticised for putting money and material success before God. He knows that he has ignored God. He also knows that God still loves him, but he recognises the distance he has put between himself and God. He very much regrets his failings and therefore goes to the priest, confesses his sins and is absolved. He goes away content and at peace, knowing that because of the priest's absolution he can start again, and that his sins are forgiven by God.

The big difference between this model and Model 2 is that this one involves the creator God whilst Model 2 was relevant to the anti-realist's God.

In this model, praying for forgiveness (i) has the same psychological effects as in Model 1, although the priest is necessary here to reassure the individual. In addition, (ii) the priest is the person who reconciles the individual to his or her community, which was a feature of Model 2(a). Also, (iii) the priest reconciles the individual to the creator God. It is important to notice, that in this view, reconciliation to the creator God takes place through the offices of the priest.

This view is a much more Catholic approach than the alternative below, which sees little role for the priest. The Catholic Church still insists on its members going to a priest for individual confession and absolution. The Catholic will go to confession, the priest will give penance and will then absolve the individual of his or her sins – although genuine repentance is a necessary precondition for absolution.

In the Anglican Church, in which personal confessions are rare, only the priest can pronounce the absolution of sins, although the differences in wording between the occasions

when the priest takes the service and when a lay reader takes it
is a very small one. The priest will say:

> *Almighty God, who forgives all who truly repent,*
> *have mercy upon you,*
> *pardon and deliver you from all your sins,*
> *confirm and strengthen you in all goodness,*
> *and keep you in life eternal,*
> *through Jesus Christ our Lord. Amen.*

(Alternative Service Book 1980, p. 62)

A lay person taking the service will use precisely the same
words, except that "you" will be changed to "us". The
alteration is significant. The use of "you" means that on
behalf of the creator God the priest is forgiving those
attending the service. The use of "we" means that all those
attending the service are, together, coming before God to
seek his forgiveness. The Anglican approach is to accept both
models.

Model 4

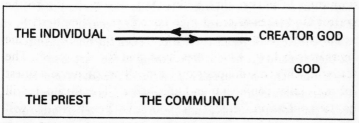

Karen knows that God loves her and is her friend, but she also
knows that the way she has acted has been appalling. She has
ignored God, turned her back on her friend, acted in ways
that deliberately shut Him out of her life. She knows that God
still loves her and she speaks to Him in her prayer, saying how

sorry she is for all the things she has done. She knows that her true happiness can only be found in re-establishing her relationship with God, which has been broken by her actions. She resolves anew to only act in such a way as God would approve of. She will show love, she will not be impatient, she will be less selfish. Having prayed, Karen feels and knows that God has forgiven her. She goes on her way refreshed and relaxed, secure in her relationship with God.

In this more typically Protestant view Karen, in praying for forgiveness, is seeking to re-establish her relationship with the creator God. She has sinned and has turned away from Him, as if from a friend. The relationship of love – the two-way I/Thou relationship that should exist between the believer and the creator God – has been spoilt by her actions. Of course, God's love for Karen has not changed, but she has herself undermined the relationship. In praying for forgiveness, she is therefore recognising the breakdown in the relationship that has taken place and is seeking to re-establish the previous ties of love and friendship.

The closest parallel to this is my hurting a friend by some word or action. Because I have hurt him I have placed a barrier between myself and my friend. I can go to him and say: "I'm sorry. I shouldn't have done that. I recognise that I have hurt you. Because I care for you I regret what I have done. Please, will you forgive me?" Then the relationship will be mended and the hurt will be a thing of the past. So it is with God. The believer goes to God, as if to a friend, to re-establish the lost relationship. He or she will be secure in the knowledge that forgiveness is available. After all, even good human friends can forgive, and God's love is much greater than that of any human. However, the believer will know that it is he or she who must move to re-establish the broken relationship. The person has turned away from God, and only he or she can choose to turn back again.

You will notice that the diagram above, unlike the diagram for Model 3, has an arrow coming back from God to the individual. This is necessary, because the creator God is held to respond to the individual who prays in much the same way as a friend would respond. Crucial to this model is the idea of a two-way personal relationship which is not a feature of Model 1 or Model 2 and which is less strongly emphasised in Model 3.

Vincent Brummer (*What Are We Doing When We Pray?*, SCM Press 1984) helpfully discusses this fourth model of petitionary prayer. He draws a useful distinction between (i) an understanding of God's relation to the individual believer based on the idea of a two-way relationship or fellowship and (ii) an understanding based on the idea of a contractual obligation or agreement. Brummer clearly favours the former model. He writes:

> Whereas broken fellowship can only be restored by penitence and forgiveness, broken agreements are restored by satisfaction, punishment or condonation. If we do not clearly distinguish agapeistic fellowship from an agreement of rights and duties, we will also tend to confuse penitence with punishment and forgiveness with condonation . . .
>
> Penitential prayers in which we confess our sins to God and ask his forgiveness, presuppose that the God to whom we pray is a personal Being with whom we may enter into a personal relationship . . . If we were to interpret the relation between God and human persons in terms of rights and duties, this would either make prayers for divine forgiveness inappropriate, or turn them into acts which somehow merit the restoration of one's rights before God, or into requests for divine condonation or remission of penalty . . .

Brummer's point is significant. He is claiming that the believer's relationship with God can be looked at in two ways:

1. The believer's relationship with God can be regarded as being a contractual one, with punishment and penalties being imposed for infringement of the terms of the agreement. The believer is required to live up to certain standards set by God – he or she must develop the full potential of his or her human nature. Failure to do this will result in punishment – the most extreme forms of which are very nasty indeed. Brummer considers that this is a mistaken view, albeit one that is widely held.

2. Instead Brummer considers that we should look at the relationship between God and believer as a two-way love-relationship. On this view, prayer for forgiveness involves seeking to re-establish a relationship that has been spoilt.

On this view, no priest is necessary. I do not have to go to a third party if I have hurt my friend – I go to him directly. Similarly, if the believer has sinned, he can go straight to God and seek His forgiveness. The psychological benefits to the individual seeking forgiveness are undoubted, but these effects come from feeling that the God-relationship has been restored. It is not simply a meditative technique.

This approach sees no real place for the community in praying for forgiveness, except in so far as all believers who belong to a community may recognise their own failures, fallibility and sinfulness and see themselves as fellow pilgrims on the road towards God. There is no particular need for each individual to be reconciled back into the community, because the community consists of individuals who are all sinners. They do not consider that failure or sin places the individual outside the community in such a way that he or she needs to be accepted back in once more.

* * *

All the four models we have considered are viable possibilities, although we have seen that they have different implications. It is hard to say that one is more plausible than another on philosophic grounds – once the different presuppositions are accepted. The key issue is this: which presuppositions are valid?

1. Does God exist as timeless substance or everlasting spirit – is God, in other words, the traditional creator God? If the answer is "No", then either Model 1 or Model 2 (a and b) will apply; if it is "Yes", then either Model 3 or Model 4 apply.

2. Does the believer have to be reconciled to his or her community in any formal way after committing sins? If the answer is "No", then either Model 1 or Model 4 will apply; if it is "Yes", then either Model 2 or Model 3 will apply.

3. Is a priest necessarily a part of the individual being forgiven? If the answer is "No", then either Model 1, Model 2(b) or Model 4 will apply; if it is "Yes", then either Model 2(a) or Model 3 will apply.

The choices are ours to make – although we should recognise that these choices should involve some rational grounds. Therefore, before we choose which model of prayer for forgiveness to adopt we should give further careful consideration to the presuppositions.

Summary

We have analysed four possible ways in which believers understand praying for forgiveness. They are all rational and plausible, depending on which of the underlying preconceptions about (i) God, (ii) the believer's community and (iii) the role of the priest are adopted. The different variables have been set out immediately above.

At the least, prayer is a meditative exercise with therapeutic effects. It may also involve reconciliation of the individual with the community to which he or she belongs. In addition, if God is held to exist as timeless substance or an everlasting spirit, praying for forgiveness may involve reconciliation of the individual to the creator God.

SEVENTEEN

Miracles

Jesus is claimed to have turned water into wine; to have walked on water; to have fed five thousand people on five loaves and two fishes; to have raised Lazarus from the dead; to have cured a woman with a haemorrhage; to have restored people's sight; to have cured leprosy; to have made the lame walk; and, after being killed, to have risen from the dead on Easter Sunday. The Gospels are full of accounts of miracles. If one is going to take the gospel writers at all seriously, then the miracle stories cannot be too quickly dismissed.

However, the Bible does not provide a very clear starting point. Biblical scholars consider that some of the stories in the New Testament may have been added later on; others may have been exaggerated accounts. And even if the accounts are true, this does not necessarily mean that miracles of this type occur today. Also, the Bible acknowledges that miracles can be performed not only by followers of the true God – the magicians who served Pharaoh could perform miracles just as impressive as those performed by Moses.

What does it mean to talk about miracles? Here are some of the various possible definitions:

1. A miracle is a change for the better that can take place in a person in even the most unlikely situation.

2. A miracle is an event or occurrence which the believer considers to have religious significance, even though it is

not in fact due to the creator God.

3. A miracle is an event caused by the action of an everlasting or timeless God. The event is either in accordance with the normal laws of nature, or else brought about by a human being, in which case God will be the primary cause whilst the person will be the secondary cause.

4. A miracle is an event which happens against the laws of nature, and which is brought about by the action of the everlasting or timeless God.

Much depends on whether God is in any sense an agent who can act in the world. We saw in Chapter Fourteen that there is much dispute as to whether it makes sense to claim that timeless God is capable of acting in the world. Many modern philosophers have claimed that timeless action is impossible, but we saw that their accounts are flawed. Timeless action, if properly understood, is not necessarily against the laws of logic. For the purpose of our discussion of miracles, therefore, we shall assume that God as timeless substance or as an everlasting spirit is capable of acting and intervening in the world which He has created and now sustains.

Let us now consider the possibilities:

A miracle as a change for the better in a person

In Dostoyevsky's *The Brothers Karamazov* we read of Alyosha, a young and holy monk who is studying under the elder monk, Zossima. In the town near the monastery is a lady of somewhat lax morals called Grushenka who has had her eyes on Alyosha but who has made no progress with him at all. Then Zossima dies, and the monastic community and the people from the village gather round his bed. The expectation in Russia at this time is that if a very holy person dies, his or her body will not decompose. So for three days those around the bed of the dead Zossima wait patiently. Eventually it becomes obvious that there is a smell – Zossima's body is decomposing. Alyosha is devastated. The man whom he has looked up to and revered was obviously not as holy as he thought. Alyosha leaves the monastery and finds his way to Grushenka's house. He is totally vulnerable, and one expects Grushenka to comfort him in her own way. Instead, Grushenka puts Alyosha together spiritually – the transformation in her is quite remarkable. It is transformations such as this, in possibly the most unlikely people and situations, that Sutherland regards as truly being miracles.

Sutherland wants to claim that human beings are free and always have the capacity for great good. The ability of the good to break through in any situation is where the true power of miracle lies.

This view of miracle does not demand a creator God and is a view that can be held by supporters of any of the four views of God that we have been examining. Supporters of God as an everlasting spirit or as timeless substance may ascribe the transformation in a human being to the power of God – although if they do this, they will have to be careful to ensure that their interpretation of God's action does not undermine human freedom.

A miracle as an event which believers consider to have religious significance, even though it is not in fact due to the creator God

On this definition of miracle, any event – not just a transformation in a human being – which is seen by a believer or a group of believers as having religious significance would be termed a miracle. Such events will not go against natural laws but will instead be "disclosure events" – they will disclose to believers something about God or the nature of reality. Thus the night sky, the opening of a spring flower, the wonder of a baby's first cry, the love between two people or the beauty of the earth seen from space can all be regarded as miraculous.

On this view, whether or not something is a miracle depends entirely on how event(s) are seen by different believers. This is an anti-realist view – the term "miracle" is correctly applied if the word makes sense within the form of life of the religious believer. The term does not have to correspond to any particular state of affairs in order to be correctly applied (it is this factor that distinguishes this approach from that taken under the next heading). It follows, therefore, that one person may see something as a miracle whilst to another it may be no more than the normal unfolding of the world according to determined rules. To one, the night sky may be seen as the hand of God and may bring this person to look at the whole of his or her life in a new way. He or she may come to reject concern with wealth and the normal goals in life and may instead seek to live a life of self-sacrificial love. To another person, the night sky is merely the reflection of sunlight slanting through the earth's atmosphere by specks of dust blown by the wind. Both views may be held to be right, within their different forms of life.

The Dominican priest, Gareth Moore, in his book *Believing in God – a Philosophical Essay* (T. & T. Clarke, 1989) has produced an interesting view of miracle which could be included under this heading. His approach is based on Wittgenstein's philosophy and he is firmly committed to the view that God is nothing. This is not a restatement of Aquinas' view that God is no thing, but rather a commitment to the view that the word "God" does not refer to any being at all. God is not an agent who created and sustains the universe. For Moore, a miracle occurs where there is no explanation – it is specifically not an act of a creator God. He says of a typical cure obtained at Lourdes:

> Much of the investigation is concerned with ruling out possible causes for the cure, showing what has not caused it; and it is certainly not proved to be a miracle by the discovery of the cause for the cure and its subsequent identification as God (p. 226) . . .
>
> To say that God brought it about is not to say that *somebody* brought it about . . . God causes what *nothing* causes (p. 223).

If, therefore, we have a situation where there is no explanation at all, the believer will rightly call this a miracle, whilst the non-believer will say that the phenomenon merely has no explanation. The non-believer, "who has no context available to him to fit the event into, therefore simply finds it baffling" (p. 225). The believer "does believe that God is responsible for it, but to believe that is not to believe that *somebody* is responsible for it" (p. 225). The believer has a context, a form of life and a language with which to explain events that the non-believer describes as inexplicable. Whereas the non-believer uses terms such as "baffling", the believer uses terms such as "God" and "miracle".

For Moore, God is not an agent, and so in his view it is wrong to think of miracles as events brought about by a creator God who acts in the world.

Moore's account is interesting and it makes sense, given the anti-realist position (we must remember Moore's maxim, given in the final sentence of his book: 'People do not discover religious truths, they make them" (p. 287)). However, his account depends on God *not* being timeless substance or an everlasting spirit, since both these are agents who can and do bring about effects in the universe which they are held to have created and to still sustain. If "God exists" is true within the form of life of the believing community, or if language about God tells us something about a different way in which we can live life, then Moore's account may be plausible – although it does confine miracle to the realm of bizarre happenings.

Moore points out that miracles generally only occur as a result of a series of disasters. If God really is an agent of some sort, why does He allow situations to arise which make it necessary for miracles to be performed, so that things can be put right? To think of miracles as actions by God is in effect to say that this agent God has made a mess of the series of events which has led up to the present need for a miracle.

For Moore, as an anti-realist, a miracle is not an action by an agent God – it is an event which has no explanation at all. That is what the word "miracle" means. This is an attractive view, but many believers would want to reject Moore's thesis and to claim that miracles *are* actions by an agent God who brings about effects in the world. Those who hold this view would opt for the third or fourth of our accounts of what it means to talk of a miracle.

A miracle as an event caused by an everlasting or timeless God which is either in accordance with the known laws of nature or else brought about by human beings

This view is very similar to the preceding one. However, whilst that was an anti-realist approach to miracle, this is a realist understanding. On this view, an event is only correctly described as a miracle if, and only if, it is brought about by the action of an everlasting or timeless God. The believer may claim that an event is a miracle on exactly the same basis as above, but what will make this claim true or false is whether or not the creator God *did*, in fact, bring about the state of affairs.

Since the believer can neither point to any event which goes against any known law of nature nor prove that the event was caused by God, his or her claim is going to remain at the level of a faith claim. However, the claim may be true – but only if the event described as a miracle actually *is* brought about by God. Since there is no way of conclusively proving or disproving this, the claim will be one made and supported by faith alone. In this sense, the parallels with the preceding view are very close.

Miracles under this heading do not transgress the laws of nature – they may be just part of the normal, natural order of the world or they may be cases where God seems to act through a human being (Aquinas' principle of "double agency" – see pp. 153f – would be relevant here). Such miracles could, therefore, be identical to the examples we have previously looked at (the night sky, the opening of a spring flower, a baby's first cry, etc.). The difference here is that the believer claiming a miracle under this heading is specifically claiming that the event in question is being brought about by the action of God. It is not just a "disclosure event" which is being seen in a certain way by the believer. God, on this view, is an agent who acts in the world.

The best-known example of such a providential miracle may be that described by R. F. Holland (*American Philosophical Quarterly*, 1965, p. 43). Imagine a child whose toy car has become stuck on a level crossing. The mother sees the child and also sees that an express train is hurtling towards the crossing. Suddenly, the train's emergency brakes are applied and it shudders to a halt only a short distance from the child. The mother utters a prayer of thanks to God for this miracle. However, subsequent investigation shows that the driver fainted. The faint was explainable on routine medical grounds, without any recourse to divine intervention. The mother, however, in spite of the medical explanation that is given to her, never ceases to believe that God acted to stop the train in order to save her child. This miracle – if miracle it indeed was – is not against the laws of nature. Instead, God is held to have acted through the laws of nature.

What we have here is the difference between the realist and the anti-realist understanding. The realist claims that the word "miracle" is correctly applied if and only if the event is brought about by the action of God – in the case of Holland's example, if and only if the driver's faint was caused by God. The anti-realist holds that the word "miracle" is correctly applied if it coheres with the understanding of miracle within the religious form of life of the mother. The anti-realist would claim that it would be true to describe the event as a miracle if this made sense within the mother's form of life. The dividing line is a fine one. It can be spelt out more clearly by means of these two statements:

1. "This event is a miracle because, although it is in accordance with natural law, it has particular religious significance."

2. "This event is a miracle because it is brought about by a specific action on the part of the timeless or everlasting God."

The realists (i.e. those who advocate the view of miracle given under the present heading, are committed to *both* statements 1. *and* 2. The anti-realists (i.e. those who advocate the view of miracle given under the previous heading) are only committed to statement 1.

On both understandings of miracle, any event may be described as miraculous and much is going to depend on "the eye of the beholder". There is no point in looking for further evidence to help us decide between the realist and anti-realist interpretations. There is no disagreement about the facts; the evidence is not in dispute. The disagreement is about how these facts are interpreted and what it means to claim that it is true that a miracle has occurred.

A miracle as an event which happens against the laws of nature, and which is brought about by the action of the everlasting or timeless God

David Hume's definition of a miracle is clear and to the point. A miracle is: "A transgression of a law of nature by a particular volition of the Deity, or by the interposition of some invisible agent." This is the classic understanding of a miracle, and many readers of this chapter will probably have been saying of the definitions so far: "Yes, these are all well and good, but none of these are *real* miracles." The miracles in the New Testament (walking on water, turning water into wine, healings, the raising of Lazarus) all seem to fit into this category. God, or Jesus – to the Christian believer the two are, for the purposes of miracle, more or less interchangeable – acted and breached the normal understanding of natural law. His power to walk on water showed His mastery over the physical elements. God still intervenes today.

We do have a fairly accurate understanding of natural laws. To be sure, some of our ideas may be inaccurate, but on the whole we know the ways in which many of the natural laws operate. Richard Swinburne claims that we are justified in taking an event to be a violation of natural law if it is inconsistent with our whole understanding of the scheme of things. He says:

> We have to some extent good evidence about what are the laws of nature, and some of them are so well established and account for so much data that any modification of them

which we could suggest to account for the odd counter-instance would be so clumsy and ad hoc as to upset the whole structure of science.

(*The Concept of Miracle*, p. 32)

Examples such as walking on water, the Resurrection and turning water into wine would seem to fit in well with Swinburne's understanding of a breach of natural law. To expect us to revise our understanding of natural law because of a single reported instance of someone walking on water seems unreasonable in the extreme.

There are real problems as to whether the classic under-standing of a miracle should be accepted, and we are going to have to devote more attention to this definition of miracle than to any other. Two attacks on this definition need to be taken very seriously.

David Hume

Hume's rejection of miracles is a classic piece of philosophic writing and is often quoted. His attack on reports of miracles is clear and sustained. Hume asks us, as rational human beings, to balance on the one hand the improbability of miracles occurring and on the other hand the evidence that they have occurred. He claims that, if we do this, we will always come to the conclusion that it is more likely that natural laws have held good rather than that a miracle has occurred. Here is a paraphrase of Hume's argument:

A wise man proportions his belief to the evidence. A miracle is the violation of the laws of nature and is therefore an event which past human experience is uniformly against. This in itself makes it overwhelmingly probable that the miracle did not occur, unless the testimony to its occurrence is of such superlative quality that it can seriously be weighed against our own uniform past experience.

In fact, however, the testimony to miracles is not of this character at all. The standard of the witnesses to miracles is not high. The human capacity for accepting or believing the unlikely has all too probably been at work, the stories of miracles derive from "ignorant and barberous places and nations" and, in any case, the miracle stories of different religions contradict each other. Consequently testimony to miracles can never establish them so that one could proceed from a proper assurance that they occurred to infer some theistic conclusions.

This is a famous statement and it is worth examining the claims Hume is making in some detail. He argues:

1.   A miracle is a breach of a law of nature – an example would be a man walking on water, or water being changed into wine.

2.   Belief in miracles is not rational. For Hume, rationality involves the following principles:

   – Proportioning our belief to the evidence available.
   – Accepting that we have uniform past evidence for laws of nature. All our experience tells us that when people walk on water they sink; that the molecular structure of water cannot change into that of wine; that once someone has died, they do not rise from the dead.

It will always, Hume argues, be more rational to believe that the laws of nature continue to hold and that no miracles have occurred.

3.   Not only is belief in miracles (defined as breaches of the

laws of nature) irrational, but the testimony available is poor. Thus:

– The testimony of witnesses is unreliable and untrustworthy. Hume says that a rational man would expect witnesses, if they were going to be considered to be reliable, to be educated and intelligent. They should have a reputation to lose and nothing to gain. In the case, for instance, of the New Testament miracle stories, the relatively ignorant fisherman had a great deal to gain from miracle stories which would make their master appear in a good light.

– Human nature loves the fantastic. People love the idea of something unlikely happening. Many still claim to have experienced Unidentified Flying Objects and others claim to see the Loch Ness monster. Some people lie, whilst many others are sincerely mistaken.

– Generally, reports of miracles come from ignorant and barbarous people. Primitive folklore has many tales of miracles and strange stories of the supernatural.

If, therefore, the poor testimony to miracles is put together with the unlikelihood that laws of nature have been breached, it will always be more sensible to reject reports of miracles than to believe them. This is, Hume considers, the obvious conclusion to be reached if we weigh the evidence on both sides.

4. All religions claim miracles, so therefore all religions have equal claims to truth, if one bases the truth of those religions on the miracle stories. Assuming that different religions are not compatible, their differing miracle stories

simply cancel out and provide, as Hume puts it, a "complete triumph for the sceptic".

All in all, therefore, Hume maintains that it should never be rational to believe in reports of miracles.

Hume's argument has much to commend it, but if we examine his claims in closer detail, their effectiveness will be seen to be more limited than he may have imagined.

1. Hume talks of "laws of nature" as if they were set in stone, thus implying that no natural law can ever be shown to be false. However, science advances by showing that our existing understandings of some natural laws are incorrect. Otherwise one would have to ignore any experiments that showed our present theories to be false. To be fair to Hume, he could restate his point here and maintain that one should only take account of evidence against a supposed natural law if this evidence could be duplicated under controlled laboratory conditions and had predictive power. In other words, one should ignore what appear to be isolated exceptions to breaches of natural law, and should only take account of exceptions if an experiment which showed the natural law to be false could be repeated. The possibility must remain open, however, for laws of nature to be shown to be false – and this is something that Hume does not recognise.

2. Hume only deals with reports of miracles. Nothing in his argument shows that one should ignore a miracle that one has experienced oneself. If Hume himself had experienced a miracle, he might well have believed it – even if he insisted on rejecting any second-hand reports.

3. Hume was writing at a time when the only support for miracle stories came from word-of-mouth reports. Today,

claimed miracles are sometimes supported by scientific evidence. At Lourdes there have been seventy carefully attested claims that miracles have occurred (apart from many other claims which have not received the authentication of the Church). The evidence has been carefully sifted and documented by unbiased scientists working with the latest available medical equipment. Bones have re-grown when all the evidence is that this cannot happen; terminal cancers have gone into permanent remission and many other inexplicable events have been clearly proved. Here, the doctors are exactly of the sort that Hume demanded – they have reputations to lose and the evidence is incontrovertible.

4.   Neither Christianity, Islam nor Judaism has ever claimed that someone should believe on the basis of miracles. Jesus himself rejected any appeal to signs and wonders as evidence for his status. He rejected the Devil's temptation in the wilderness to perform a miracle by throwing himself down from the Temple, and also the temptation to miraculously save himself from the cross. When, therefore, a person considers whether belief in miracles is rational or not, he or she does not have to look on them as an unbiased observer. If someone believes in the existence of God on other grounds, it may therefore be rational to believe that God acts in the world to suspend natural law. What is *not* rational is to believe in any particular religion on the basis of reports of miracles. In this, at least, Hume's arguments appear convincing.

Although the evidence for extraordinary events at places like Lourdes is good, this does not prove that the extraordinary events have been brought about by the agency of God. Perhaps, instead, we may be dealing with evidence of the remarkable power of the human mind. A hundred years ago, video cameras, portable televisions and cellular radios would have been considered miraculous, yet they are part of today's routine technology. Similarly, psychology has helped us to understand much about the mind which has previously been wrapped in mystery.

There is a great deal that we do not know about the human mind. It may well be possible that, under the right conditions, our minds can bring about changes in our bodies. Perhaps the remarkable events at Lourdes and at other places may be due to the psychosomatic effect of the human mind. Much will depend on the individual's prior presuppositions. If a person believes in a God who acts in the world, then it is possible that he or she may hold that such a God has intervened to bring about a miracle. If another person has no such belief, then there is no need to attribute inexplicable events to the agency of God.

However, another challenge now awaits those who consider that miracles represent acts by a divine agent against the laws of nature. This challenge is more devastating and effective than that of Hume and it is put forward by a modern philosopher – Maurice Wiles.

Maurice Wiles

Wiles' proposal in *God's Action in the World* (SCM Press, 1986) is that "the primary usage for the idea of divine action should be in relation to the world as a whole rather than to particular occurrences within it" (p. 28). He wants to speak of "the world as a whole as a single act of God" (p. 29). He believes "there are no good grounds for speaking of particular divine actions with respect to particular phenomena" (p. 34). He is claiming, in other words, that there is a single act of God – and this act encompasses the world as a whole. God never intervenes in the world by individual acts. Wiles continues:

If the direct action of God, independent of secondary

causation, is an intelligible concept, then it would appear to have been sparingly and strangely used. Miracles must by definition be relatively infrequent or else the whole idea of laws of nature . . . would be undermined, and ordered life as we know it would be an impossibility. Yet even so it would seem strange that no miraculous intervention prevented Auschwitz or Hiroshima, while the purposes apparently forwarded by some of the miracles acclaimed in traditional Christian faith seem trivial by comparison (p. 66).

In other words, Wiles challenges the idea of a God who would intervene in the ordered universe by bringing about a few bizarre miracles against the laws of nature. He is claiming that an interventionist God is a debased idea of God – effectively a God who would not be worthy of worship.

Wiles quotes Brian Hebblethwaite, who accepts the conceivability of miracle on philosophic grounds. But he is much more dubious about whether miracles, defined as breaches of laws of nature, ever occur:

To suppose that God acts in the world by direct intervention just occasionally would be to raise all the problems which perplex the believer as he reflects on the problem of evil, about why God does not intervene more often. It would also prevent him from appealing to the God-given structures of creation, and their necessary role in setting creatures at a distance from their creator and providing a stable environment for their lives, as an explanation for the physical ills which can afflict God's creatures.

(*Evil, Suffering and Religion*, p. 92–3)

Wiles sees, therefore, "no need for the Christian believer to affirm any form of direct divine intervention in the natural order and good reasons for not doing so" (p. 69). A God that acted in some special cases and not in others would have an apparently arbitrary will, and this apparent arbitrariness would be a serious objection to the idea of miracles as direct intervention by God in the natural order. Because of this and because of Hebblethwaite's points above, Wiles wants to "deny to God the freedom to act without causal restraint in the world" (p. 80). This, he holds, does not depersonalise God at all, as the whole of creation is the act of God – which God does not act against by any form of special intervention.

The idea of an interventionist God is, Wiles maintains, "both implausible and full of difficulty for a reasoned Christian faith". He is right about the difficulties – at least if we insist on a rational understanding. A God who intervenes at Lourdes to cure an old man from terminal cancer but does not act to save starving millions in Ethiopia; who helps the individual believer by giving him or her personal guidance about whether to take a new job or to sell his or her house, but does not prevent the mass murder of the Jews at Auschwitz – such a God needs, at the least, to face some hard moral questioning. Some may hold that this God is not worthy of worship.

We must recognise that Wiles – and many contemporary theologians who have similar views – are assuming that human reason can understand the ways of God. In doing this, they are in a Kantian tradition which maintains that religion must be within the limits of reason alone. This, in itself, is an assumption. Saint Paul said that he preached "Christ cruci-fied", which was "foolishness to the Greeks". The Greeks were the philosophers of St Paul's day, and it may well be that some of today's philosophers, by affirming the supremacy of human reason, reduce Christianity to a human construct. Any creator God may, just possibly, lie beyond the appre-hension of human beings.

Summary

We have looked at four possible definitions of miracle:

1. A miracle as a change for the better that can take place in a human person in the most unlikely situation.

2. A miracle as an event or occurrence which the believer considers to have religious significance but which is not brought about by an agent God.

3. A miracle as an event which is brought about by the action of an everlasting or timeless God, but which is either in accordance with the normal laws of nature, or is an event brought about by a human being of which God is primary cause whilst the person is the secondary cause.

4. A miracle as an event against the laws of nature brought about by the action of the everlasting or timeless God.

The last two of these possibilities will be confined to believers in an everlasting or timeless God who can act in the world.

The definition of miracle as a breach of natural law suffers particular problems when it forms part of a rational Christian faith. If miracles are arbitrary or inexplicable acts against the laws of nature by an agent God, then there are real moral questions to be asked about whether this is a God worthy of worship. Some believers may maintain, however, that they still want to affirm the existence of the creator God and the ability of this God to act in the world – even if they cannot understand the basis on which this God chooses to act.

EIGHTEEN

Eternal Life

He has made everything beautiful in its time:
Also he has put eternity into man's mind,
Yet so that he cannot find out what God has done
from the beginning to the end.

(Ecclesiastes 3:11)

The view one takes of God will largely determine the view
one takes of what it means to talk about eternal life. There are
two main possibilities:

1. Eternal life as a different quality of life here and now, in
   this world.
2. Eternal life as a different quality of life here and now, in
   this world, as well as a personal survival of death.

Eternal life as a different quality of life

Religious believers have too often stressed the idea of eternal
life as something that occurs at death. However, the Christian
tradition has always maintained that there is more to it than
this. Eternal life involves a change in the way the individual
lives. Believers talk of a "new birth" into a new way of
looking at and approaching life. Suddenly the priorities
shared by so many people in the world no longer seem
important, and life takes on a different quality. It is no longer
power, money or material possessions that matter, but rather

compassion, love, relationships with people and the higher values. As the Danish philosopher and theologian Soren Kierkegaard put it in *Purity of Heart* (Harper and Row, 1948):

> Immortality cannot be a final alteration that crept in, so to speak, at the moment of death as the final stage. On the contrary, it is a changelessness that is not altered by the passage of the years . . . If there is something eternal in a man it must be able to exist and be grasped within every change (pp. 35–36).

Christianity has always maintained that man can "live in the eternal" in this world (the quotes from John's Gospel on page 55 bear this out).

The Christian revisionists, whether they be realists or anti-realists, all talk of eternal life solely as a different quality of life here and now. They dismiss belief in a life after death or, in Sutherland's case, are agnostic about the possibility and consider it to be irrelevant. By living the holy life, we are enabled to overcome trivialisation, and to be grounded in the eternal or to live life *sub specie aeternitatis*. D. Z. Phillips maintains that the eternal quality of an individual's life is its timeless quality of moral excellence. Talk of the immortality of the soul refers to a person's relation to the self-effacement and love of others involved in dying to the self – it does not refer to *post-mortem* existence.

The person whose inner life is orientated correctly, who is with passion and commitment seeking to live the good life, seeking to be kind, compassionate and gentle and to live for others is, no matter what happens, invulnerable. He or she is "living in the eternal" and cannot be harmed, as nothing can take away this inner orientation. However things go in the world, the person whose life is grounded in the eternal cannot be overcome.

It is important to recognise that the idea of eternal life as a different quality of life now is common to all Christians – whatever the view of God to which they subscribe. Many, however, want to say more than this.

Eternal life as the timeless Beatific Vision

We have previously seen that Roman Catholic theology affirms that God is outside time and outside space. This has important implications for the way that Catholic theologians look at life after death.

Saint Thomas Aquinas used Aristotle's idea of the separation of soul and body to explain the nature of human beings. For Aquinas, the *soul* is an individual *spiritual substance* (in other words, it can exist by itself), but it is also the form of the whole body. In Aristotelian philosophy, the form of a thing is that which remains unchanged in spite of the outward changes. Thus the form of "treeness" would remain unchanged in spite of the changes in an individual tree. Aquinas considered that both body and soul together were needed to make a full human person, although the soul can survive death by itself.

Many people misunderstand Aquinas here. Aquinas and the Catholic Church, which has largely followed him, do *not* say that a person is made up of a soul and a body, and that after death the soul, which is the real person, survives. This is a straightforward *dualist* view. (A dualist holds that a human person is made up of two separate components – soul and body – which are independent of each other and yet interact in this world.) The dualist approach means that our identity lies in our soul, whilst our bodies are almost irrelevant. Plato was a dualist, and this led him to have a fairly low opinion of human bodies and the physical world as a whole, as the ultimate destiny for man was for the "real me" to survive death as a disembodied soul. This is not the view of Aquinas nor that of the Catholic Church.

In Aquinas' view, soul and body are both needed to make a full human individual. The soul is in the body, just as God is present throughout the world. Aquinas says: ". . . all man's soul is in all his body and again all of it is in any part of his body, in the same way as God is in the world" (*Summa Theologica* 1a, 93 3). The soul is present in every part of the body; it is not a "separate something", hidden away somewhere, which somehow interacts with the body.

Aquinas held that, when we die, our souls survive and go either to hell or to purgatory or to the Beatific Vision (there is another destination, limbo – which I will not deal with here). It is important to be clear on the difference between these:

1. Hell is temporal – in other words, time passes in hell. Aquinas maintained that those destined for hell suffer exclusion from God's presence and also eternal torment, pain and punishment. This punishment continues for ever and ever, as the human body could not stand the pain required if the period were to be shorter and the pain more intense. Modern writers tend to play down the punishment side of hell and instead see it as the place to which those people go who have deliberately, out of self-will, turned away from God.

2. Most souls pass to purgatory. Purgatory is the place, Catholic theology maintains, where individuals undergo purification and punishment pending their entry into their final end. It is, effectively, a "holding state" where the soul is purged of the sins committed on earth. Only the wholly perfected and worthy souls are fit for the Beatific Vision. Purgatory is temporal – time passes there. Aquinas held that, after death, the guilt of venial sin is done away with by God by an act of pure charity. But the individual still has to

undergo the punishment for his or her sins. The smallest pain in purgatory is greater than the greatest pain on earth, but the pain in purgatory is relieved because everyone who goes there knows that they will eventually pass to the Beatific Vision of God which is held to be the highest joy. Today less emphasis tends to be placed on the punishment that takes place in purgatory and more on the growth and development that may take place. Also, Catholic theology has moved away from speaking too literally about the number of days of relief from pain and suffering in purgatory that can be gained for oneself or others through good works.

There is, however, a problem. The soul goes to purgatory, but Aquinas specifically says, *"Anima mea non est ego"* ("my soul is not I"). As we have seen above, a human person is the unity of body and soul. Aquinas considers that all those in purgatory receive a new and glorified body at some time when their sins have been sufficiently cleansed. The problem is this: If I am in purgatory and it is my soul that is in purgatory, then I must be my soul. However, Aquinas says that I am not my soul – or at least, my soul is not fully me. Now either Peter Vardy is in purgatory or he is not. If he is, then Peter Vardy is his soul. And yet Aquinas denies this.

What is more, surely the pains and punishment that the individual has to undergo in purgatory require a body so that they can be experienced. Individual souls, however, have no bodies in purgatory.

Aquinas says that the soul is not "fully me", and the real issue is whether we can make sense of this. Can the "I" which I am now, be only partly this "I" in Purgatory until it acquires a new and glorified body? Can I be only partly me?

When the punishment/perfection in purgatory has been completed, the souls that are there receive a new and glorified body and this is in preparation for –

3. The timeless Beatific Vision. According to Catholic teaching, this is the final end for man. This Beatific Vision may vary between individuals, but it is completely satisfying. In this vision, we will share God's knowledge (except for God's motives and intentions, to which we shall not have access). As the Beatific Vision is timeless, it will never, never, ever change – it is the unchanging vision of God. There is therefore, no idea here of a heavenly society in which Aunt Mabel may meet Uncle Fred.

This idea of the timeless Beatific Vision may well have been influenced by Plato's belief that the final end for human beings was the contemplation of unchangeable Beauty, which was one of the Forms (see p. 25).

The problem with this view is that Aquinas holds that the soul receives a new and glorified body at the Second Coming. However if I, Peter Vardy, have a body, and if I need a body in order to be Peter Vardy, then I cannot become timeless. If I have a body, time must necessarily pass, and if time passes I cannot be timeless. There does, therefore, seem to be a real difficulty here. *Either* I have a body, in which case I cannot be timeless, *or* I become timeless, in which case I cannot have a body. Real questions arise as to whether it is Peter Vardy who is enjoying the timeless Beatific Vision.

When Jesus rose from the dead, he most certainly had a body – even though it was a special body which could pass through walls. He talked with the disciples, he ate food and was very much a temporal figure. If Jesus had retained this body, he could not have become timeless. After the Ascension, therefore, Jesus must have lost his post-Resurrection body in order to become the timeless Second Person of the Trinity.

There is one reply that the Catholic theologian could make – that is to claim that the new and glorified body is not to be understood univocally, but is rather a body in an analogous sense. It is true that human beings who reach the timeless Beatific Vision will have a body, but we do not know what it means for them to have a body. This, obviously, means that there is very little content indeed to the claim that we are embodied, but it does at least prevent the position from being an obvious contradiction.

This approach has two major attractions. First of all, an individual's soul (which is the form of his or her whole body) survives death and therefore establishes the link between this life and the next one. Peter Vardy survives death because it is Peter Vardy's soul that survives. Secondly, this view has a final end for human beings in the timeless, Beatific Vision of God. As we have seen, however, the problems are also considerable.

Eternal life as life after death in a heavenly society

In the previous section we considered one way of looking at a human being which might give content to talk of our surviving death – that is, if the soul is the form of the whole body. There are, however, two alternatives which are often adopted by Protestant theologians who usually – although not always – work with an everlasting rather than a timeless view of God. Both alternatives involve a heavenly society of some sort, but they differ because there are two possible understandings of what it means to be a human person.

Soul/body dualism
Straightforward soul/body dualism – which we defined in the previous section – is the model of personhood favoured by both Plato and Descartes. The soul is the real me and it is trapped in the body, which it drives like a ghost in a machine (as Gilbert Ryle puts it in his book, *The Concept of Mind*,

which rejected this view). Those who maintain that soul and mind (the two are not necessarily the same) are distinct have different ideas about their inter-relationship. Possibilities include:

1.   The idea that souls are pre-existent and survive death, passing, perhaps, to a different realm before being united to a new body. Wordsworth captured something of the flavour of a pre-existent soul in his poem, *Intimations of immortality from recollections of early childhood*:

> *Our birth is but a sleep and a forgetting;*
> *The soul that rises with us, our life's star,*
> *hath had elsewhere its setting*
> *and cometh from afar:*
> *Not in entire forgetfullness*
> *and not in utter nakedness*
> *but trailing clouds of glory do we come,*
> *from God who is our home . . .*

2.   *Creationism*, which is the belief that each soul is created by God and attached to the growing foetus at a certain point. This is one reason why some believers become so concerned about embryo research. These are, however, problems as to when God implants this soul. Up to fourteen days after the sperm and the egg unite to form a single unit (when the hair-line appears), this unit may divide and may then come together again. If, therefore, the soul is implanted by God at the moment of conception, then what happens when the unit divides? Do we then have two souls? If so, what happens if and when the two parts come together again?

3.   *Traducianism*, which is the belief that a soul is created naturally when a man and woman make love as part of

normal conception. This latter theory was developed by some of the Latin Church Fathers, such as Tertullian, who saw the soul as the substance which God breathed into Adam and which was passed down through the many generations of human beings by continuous division. It is now held to be a heresy.

There are severe problems with dualism, including the following:

1.   How do souls and bodies interact? Descartes maintained that the interaction was through a little gland at the back of the head called the Pineal Gland, but this has been discredited. The disembodied soul is meant to be "driving" the machine which is the body, but it is far from clear what the mechanism is which enables this to happen. Also, this whole approach tends to denigrate the value of the physical in human beings – emphasising the soul as that which is most important. It tends to point us away, therefore, from a holistic view of what it is to be a human being.

2.   What is the relation between soul and the mind/brain? We know that brain states can be affected by our bodies and that drugs can easily affect our minds. An operation can alter a person's whole personality and memory. Given that the brain is the seat of our emotions, memory and actions, does this mean that our souls are similarly affected? Could my soul possibly survive if my brain does not?

3.   In *The Concept of Mind* Gilbert Ryle rejected all talk about souls, since it was based on what he termed a "Category Mistake". He gave two examples, of which the second is the more interesting. Firstly, imagine showing a foreigner around a university. You show him the college buildings, the

chapels, the libraries, the staff and the students. He sees all this but then says: "Yes, I have seen all these things, but where is the University?" The mistake that he is making is to think that the university is something on top of all those things which he has seen.

The second example is that of a foreigner looking at a game of cricket. He sees the bowlers, the batsmen, the wicket keeper, the fielders and the umpires but then says: "I have seen all these people, but where is the team spirit?" Again, the mistake he makes is to think that "team spirit" is something on top of all those things he has seen. So, Ryle argues, it is with talk of the soul. The soul is not an extra something on top of the intentional actions of a human person. To talk of a soul is to talk about the way a person acts and responds to other people; it is not to talk of a disembodied ghost of some sort.

4.   Could one have a society of disembodied souls? H. H. Price, in an article entitled "Survival and the idea of another world" (in Donnelly's *Language, Metaphysics and Death*), invites us to imagine what such a society would be like. He thinks it would have to be an "image world" or a dream world into which we would carry our memories. We would be trapped within our memories and would thus in some ways create our own heaven or hell. We would be able to communicate telepathically with like-minded disembodied souls, but that would be all. As we would have no bodies we could not speak, hear, feel or experience in any other way. The laws operating in this *post-mortem* image world would be those of psychology rather than physics.

The picture which Price paints is conceivable, but not particularly attractive, and it would be likely to be a boring existence with little eventual point to it. There would be little that would be creative or life-giving in such a world. The individual disembodied mind would not be capable of acting in relation to its environment.

5. How could my soul be me? Peter Vardy is a living human person who has a body, a brain, sensory organs, emotions and feelings. It is not at all clear in what way a disembodied soul with none of these physical attributes could still be me.

The problems with dualism are considerable, therefore, and it is by no means the most popular of the theories currently on offer to explain what it is to be a person and what it might mean for a person to survive death. It is surprising, however, how prevalent it is amongst people who have not thought through its problems.

The person as a person
This second version of the idea of a heavenly society after death is a *monistic* view. Whereas dualism affirms that there are two separate substances – soul and body – monism claims that there is only one. It holds that a person is a person and that you cannot analyse a person into bits. We do not have a separate soul; rather, to talk of a soul is to talk of the way we act and react to other people (Gilbert Ryle, who was referred to above, is a monist). If we take a holistic view of what it is to be a person, it means that, if we are to survive death as individuals, we must survive with our present identity retained. We must survive death as persons.

Advocates of this view can still talk of a person's soul, but by this they do not mean a "separate something" mysteriously added onto his or her physical body and in some obscure way interacting with it. Talk of a person's soul is seen as a way of valuing the self. A person's individuality – his or her self or soul – is formed by interaction and relationships with others. We can, of course, turn away from the possibility of developing the spiritual side of our nature – we can become cold and hard. Someone might say, referring to a colleague at work: "She has no soul – she never cares for others. She just treats them as objects and never as individuals." On this view, talk of souls is talk about personality. A person's soul could still be seen as God-given insofar as his or her whole personality and individuality depend on God.

This monistic view immediately creates problems. If Anne dies, the person that is Anne lies dead on the floor. There is no separate soul that floats off somewhere else. Anne was a person and Anne is now dead. On the face of it, therefore, this approach seems bleak to those who advocate the idea of personal resurrection. However, the position is not as simple as this. Jesus, after all, was a person, and he died. His dead body was taken down from the cross and sealed in the tomb. Jesus was as dead as dead could be, and the disciples' faith in him was at an end. Yet Jesus rose from the dead, so it has traditionally been claimed, on Easter Sunday.,

Christianity has, since the early centuries when the beliefs of the Church were first formulated, always affirmed the resurrection of the body. This was really a quite remarkable thing for the Church to affirm. The world in which the early Christians lived was largely dominated by Greek philosophic thought and this tended, although not universally, to think in terms of the soul surviving death. It would have been so easy and so apparently logical for Christianity to take the same line. To actually claim that the body survived death in the face of the very clear evidence that dead bodies rotted and decayed could easily have made Christianity appear absurd.

There were various reasons for this Christian position. One of them was the belief that Jesus appeared to his disciples after his death, not as a disembodied spirit but as a resurrected person who could walk and talk with his friends and could even eat food with them. (He was, however, a special kind of person, since he could appear in a locked room.) Pre-mortem Jesus seemed remarkably similar to post-mortem Jesus, even down to the imprint of the nails in his hands.

Also, Christianity has never denied the importance of the physical world, which was a tendency of some dualist followers of Plato. The Incarnation is about God taking human flesh and making this flesh, and with it the world we live in, holy. The physical is not in some way a second class category in comparison with spiritual, disembodied souls, although it must be admitted that some Christian writers have thought in these terms.

The claim that a person survives death as an individual obviously raises the crucial issue of identity. How do we know that the Anne who dies is the same person as the Anne who rises to life again? Bernard Williams (in *Language, Metaphysics and Death*, ed. Donnelly) has argued that the one sure test of personal identity is spatio-temporal continuity. The one thing that a baby, a young girl, a mature woman and an old lady have in common is that their bodies have followed the same space/time track. The baby gradually developed over time to become the old lady. Bernard Williams' approach would clearly rule out survival of death, as the space/time track is broken by death.

John Hick (in *Death and Eternal Life*) gives several examples which he maintains count against Williams' claim. He asks us to imagine someone lecturing in London, and then suddenly disappearing, only to reappear in New York. The person's spatio-temporal time track would be broken. Most people would, however, be willing to say it was the same person if appearance, memory and other details were in all apparent respects the same. Again, if a person dies on this earth but a duplicate of him or her comes to life on the planet Juno, we should also be prepared to recognise this as being the same person. We do not need, therefore, spatio-temporal continuity in order to guarantee survival of death.

Hick considers that a person is an indissoluble psycho-physical unity. He rejects the idea of the soul as separate from the body, and with it the idea of the soul surviving death. Instead he is advancing a replica theory. The duplicate person that comes to life in heaven is an exact replica of the person who died here on earth. God is, therefore, held to create in another space an exact psycho-physical replica of the deceased Anne. This is an attractive solution, as it enables us to avoid the complexities of the relation between the soul and the body. The person who survived death would be recognisably similar to the one who died and would have the same memories as the deceased individual.

Hick does not, however, take seriously enough the distinction between (i) the same person and (ii) an identical person. The former implies a one-to-one relation between the person who has died and the person who survives. The latter, on the other hand, leaves open the possibility of a one-to-many relation. In other words, if we accept that all that is required is for a duplicate of us to be created when we die, why could not many identical copies be created? If my wife, Anne, died and a hundred duplicates were created, all looking identical and all with the same memories, I would not be able to say that any one of them was the same person as the person who had died.

Williams makes the point that memory could not count as the sole necessary criterion for identity, as we could imagine several identical bodies all being given identical memories. If someone came in claiming to be Guy Fawkes, and this person had all Guy Fawkes' memories, we would not be willing to grant that he was Guy Fawkes. If we were willing to grant this, then many people could each have the same memories, and they could not *all* be Guy Fawkes!

If we are to preserve the idea of personal survival, there

must be some criterion for establishing a one-to-one relationship between the Anne who dies and the Anne who rises from the dead. If we do not have a soul – which, of course, would neatly fulfil the task of maintaining this continuity – then there appears to be no such continuity.

In my book, *God of our Fathers* (published by Darton, Longman and Todd in 1987 but now out of print), I put forward the suggestion of a parallel between the idea of resurrection and the way my personal computer functions. In my college office I type out comments on my students' essays on this computer. These comments are stored on a computer disc. If one of my students were to lose the essay comments I could, by pressing a button, print out an identical copy. Everything on the copy would be exactly the same – spelling, phrasing, punctuation and layout. The only difference would be that the second set of essay comments would be printed on a different piece of paper to the first. If I wished, I could transmit the comments by a radio signal to a satellite. From there the signal would be bounced back to Sydney, where an identical set of comments could be printed out.

A similar process might, I argued, happen to us after death. The creator God knows each of us intimately. He knows our detailed specifications, including all our memories. So when someone dies God could, using new materials, reproduce that person. (St Paul talks of us having a new and glorified body, and there could be parallels here – possibly with defects in our bodies being rectified.) Critics will, of course, say that I have not solved the one-to-one problem. God has created an identical copy, but if He has created one copy He could create many. My critics could claim that the parallel with the computer shows my error, as I could print out as many copies of the essay comments as I wished – and they would not be the original comments.

I did, in fact, deal with this point in my original argument.

What my critics fail to take into account is that we are dealing here with God. God would simply not allow more than one Anne to be created for every Anne that died. If He did so, identity would be destroyed – and this does not happen. This still seems to me to be persuasive, although it is not foolproof. It is true that the logical possibility of duplicates remains open, but if these duplicates were created, identity would be destroyed – which is one very good reason why God would not create duplicates! It is true that, on this earth, spatio-temporal continuity may be the one sure test of identity, but this is no reason why the same test has to be applied across the boundary line of death.

On this basis, the believer could claim that the individual would survive death as an individual. The new individual would be embodied, since having a body is an integral part of my being who I am. Bodies are, however, temporal and spatial, so this view would imply that life after death is also temporal and spatial. Heaven would, on this basis, be an everlasting kingdom under the lordship of Christ. God, seen as an everlasting spirit, would be constantly present there. This would be a society filled with love and with all the negative and evil elements found in this world removed.

This world could be seen as a place where we decide what sort of people we are going to become. We can choose to make ourselves selfish, greedy and interested solely in our own pleasures. In so doing we would be turning away from God and also from love and thus place ourselves – both in this world and after death – in permanent exile from God. The contrast would be with those who seek to develop their ability to love, who seek to develop the higher virtues and who, through their actions, become people who can love and care for others. Our ultimate destiny, on this basis, lies in fellowship with God in a heavenly kingdom – but we, being free, have the right to decide whether this is the destiny we wish to choose. This is not, of course, a fashionable view, but it is a view that some Christians at least still hold, and it does not seem philosophically incoherent.

Summary

Christianity has always maintained that, at the minimum, eternal life involves a different quality of life here and now. To "live in the eternal" is to be born again into a new way of living and approaching life. Whatever view of God you adopt, this can be affirmed.

If, in addition to a different quality of life in this world, eternal life is held to involve personal survival of death, then this can take three forms:

1. Where the soul is the form of the whole body and becomes temporarily separated from the body on death, but is reunited with a new and glorious body at some time after death when the individual's sins have been purged.

2. Straightforward mind/body dualism in which the real "I" is the soul, which survives death to enter into a form of disembodied existence.

3. The view that a person dies, and later has to be resurrected. On this view there are identity problems. In particular, there is difficulty in separating the idea that the same person is resurrected from the idea that an identical copy – with the potential of many other identical copies – comes to life.

1. claims that the final end for human beings is the timeless Beatific Vision of God. 2. requires a realm of disembodied

spirits and 3. implies an everlasting spatio/temporal kingdom. None of these need be required if eternal life is only a different quality of life in this world.

NINETEEN

And So . . . ?

We have covered a lot of ground. You, the reader, are – I hope – no clearer as to where I stand* but you may be slightly surer about your own position. This is important, as you have to undertake your own search for truth. We can learn much from others but, in the end, we must make our own decisions. In these pages I have tried to present the problems involved in trying to understand the Rubik cube of God. Above all, I hope you have come to realise that there are no simple solutions and that those who are certain that they have the truth may, in all probability, not have begun to take the search for understanding seriously. As I said at the beginning, it is always easier and more comfortable to remain within the fortress of our own certainties.

Sometimes first-year undergraduate students come to me at London University very worried about all the difficulties and problems with which philosophy presents them. "You are destroying our faith by getting us to think," they sometimes say. "Why don't you give us the answers? What does the Church say?" Hopefully you, the reader, will realise the naivity of these questions – there are no simple answers and most churches have no set solutions to the problems. Indeed, the divide between the churches often saddens me because those things that divide them are often much less important

*I would personally stand behind the views expressed in my book, *And If It's True*, published by Marshall Pickering at £4.95. However, it does not solve the problems discussed in this book.

than the questions we have been here considering – yet each church contains members who hold to the views in this book.

Just how important is this debate? How important is it to be clear on which view of God we adopt? In some ways the issue does not matter at all. Supporters of all the views we have been considering maintain that the central Christian claims are true – even if their understanding of the meaning of these claims differs. Even more important, they all maintain that Christianity calls us to a different way of living life – that we are called to reject the values of materialism and our own selfish interests in favour of self-giving love for others and the path of virtue. There is a very widespread agreement between the different views about the alternative lifestyle we should adopt.

The Danish philosopher and theologian Soren Kierkegaard said: "As you have lived, so have you believed." It may well be that our lives and actions are more important than the details of our propositional beliefs. Even Jesus recognised this – he clearly said that it was not those who said, "Lord, Lord" who truly followed him, but those who looked after the sick, the imprisoned and others in need. The most intelligent philosopher does not necessarily make the best Christian – indeed, there is a real danger that preoccupation with the enjoyment of exploring ideas can lead an individual away from the life of love that the Christian path involves.

There is, therefore, a great unity between supporters of the varying views. Having said this, however, there are very significant differences as well – as we have seen during the course of this book. One way to go straight to the heart of the differences between the views we have looked at is to consider what you think happened on Easter Sunday.

Did Jesus rise from the dead after his crucifixion as an individual with his existing memories? Did Jesus literally survive death? Supporters of the different views we have looked at will answer this question in different ways:

1.   Those who believe in timeless God will maintain that Jesus did, indeed, rise from the dead as an individual. He appeared to his disciples after his death and then ascended to heaven, where he became the timeless Second Person of the Trinity. Jesus, therefore, is no longer an individual in the way he was on earth. As we have seen, timeless God has no body and is not a person or an individual as we understand the term. Rather, timeless God took flesh and became a human being and, relinquishing the flesh on his death, is once again timeless God.

2.   Those who maintain that God is everlasting will be likely to claim that Jesus did, indeed, rise from the dead as an individual. He appeared to his disciples after his death and then ascended to heaven, where he remains individual and personal – the Second Person of the tri-relational Trinity.

3.   Those who adopt Sutherland's realist view will claim that by his life Jesus actualised the way of living life *sub specie aeternitatis* which was previously a mere possibility. They will be likely to reject or possibly to remain agnostic about Jesus' survival of death, and to say that this is an issue that does not matter. They will also reject any idea of a creator God.

4.   Those who affirm the anti-realist approach will say that Jesus lived on after his death in the community of believers. Wherever two or three are gathered together in Jesus' name, there Jesus is with them. They do not, of course, affirm a creator God who is independent of the universe and yet sustains it, but will nevertheless be ready to maintain that God exists within the community of believers.

Supporters of the first two views believe in a creator God who interacts with the universe. A personal relationship between this God and the individual is, therefore, possible. Christianity is at least partly about a personal love-relationship with this God which is lived out in lives of self-giving love for those around us. They will also maintain that the individual survives death, and that men and women were created for a fellowship with God which begins on this earth but continues after death as well. Survival of death is, for them, a reality. Generally, although not always, advocates of these two views will maintain that God can act in the world, and this will influence their understanding of prayer, miracles and life after death.

These claims are not insignificant, and many believers may feel that without the constant presence of this God, the Christian life is not one that can be easily lived.

The revisionists are likely to disagree and to claim that talk of a creator God and of a relationship with this God is a relic of thinking from a bygone age. Insistence on this sort of God is now an impediment to belief and is, frankly, incredible – it is a position that can no longer be maintained in a rational and scientific world. The value, meaning and purpose of the Christian life still remains, however. Sutherland's realist view or the anti-realist revisionary review express the essential Christian truths in a way that can be credible for people living in the twenty-first century.

The debate between the different positions is likely to be long and protracted. In reading this book, you have only begun to explore the issues. I hope your reading will continue – there are suggestions for further reading in the following pages.

May whichever God you come to affirm help you in your search!

Questions for Consideration

Ch. 1. Unicorns, Numbers and God

a) What does it mean to say that God exists? Is God more like a spirit, a person, a prime number or an idea in people's minds?

b) Can it ever be right to believe in a particular way of looking at the world and not to think about one's beliefs or not to listen to other points of view?

Ch. 2. What is Truth?

a) What would one do to establish whether it is true to say "Thou shalt not steal"? Do you think the truth of this statement depends on the society in which one lives?

b) Are you a realist or an anti-realist about the future? Why?

c) If all the possible checks have been carried out to ensure that a statement is true, is it still possible that the statement could nevertheless be false? Give examples.

Ch. 3. Background to the Debate about God

a) Why was Plato's philosophy such a great influence on early Christianity?

b) Do you think Plato's idea of God conflicts with biblical ideas? Why?

c) Do you consider the straightforward biblical view or the

approach of Plato or Aristotle to God to be more compelling?

d) Could God "regret" having made the earth (Genesis Ch. 6) if this is understood in the way we normally use the word?

Ch. 4. Timeless God – a Realist View

a) Describe what it means to say that the timeless God is good.

b) If language about God was entirely equivocal, what would this mean?

c) Could one have a personal relationship with timeless God?

d) Many metaphors are used to describe God in the Bible. Find two metaphors which involve God, and which you do not think could be meant literally, and explain what you think these mean.

Ch. 5 Everlasting God – a Realist View

a) Could a God for whom time passes be worthy of worship?

b) Is it possible for a God who is in time to know the future?

c) If believers talk of having a "personal relationship with God", what do you think that they mean?

d) Select three examples from the Old or New Testaments which seem to show that God is an individual. Could these be interpreted in any other way?

Ch. 6. Talk of God as Talk about an Alternative Lifestyle – a Realist View

a) Is it correct to describe Sutherland as a realist?

b) Do you have to believe in God as the creator of the world, who is in some sense personal, in order to live a good religious life?

c) If we do not need a personal devil to explain the temptation of Jesus in the wilderness, do we need a personal God to explain Jesus' prayer in the Garden of Gethsemene?

d) Could the approach outlined in this chapter be just as relevant for Islam and Judaism as for Christianity?

e) What might be the difference between living a good moral life and living life *sub specie aeternitatis*?

Ch. 7. God as a Reality within Religious Form of Life – an Anti-Realist View

a) Are there any parallels between the existence of God and the existence of prime numbers?

b) "If there were no religious believers God would not exist." How might this view be justified?

c) Describe how you would explain the meaning of Holy Communion/The Eucharist to someone who had no knowledge of Christianity whatsoever.

d) Where did you learn about God? How big an influence do you think parents and background have on the religious beliefs that an individual may have?

e) Imagine that you had no knowledge at all of religion, describe what you would see happening in a place of worship.

Ch. 8. The Cosmological Argument

a) Is God the best explanation for the existence of the universe?

b) If God created the universe, who created God? Is this a fair question?

c) Is it reasonable that we should look for an explanation of the existence of the universe that lies outside the universe?

Ch. 9. The Ontological Argument
a) What does it mean to say that God necessarily exists?

b) What are the problems with saying that one can arrive at the existence of God by analysing God's nature?

c) Give an example of a statement that is analytically true, and another of one that is synthetically true. Describe how you would check whether both these statements are true or not.

Ch. 10. The Design Argument
a) "The beauty of the world points to the existence of a creator God." Is this claim justified?

b) If the features of the world pointed to God, what sort of God would this be?

c) Do you think that John Mill's conclusions about the results of natural theology are fair?

Ch. 11. The Argument from Religious Experience
a) How would you define a religious experience?

b) If someone claims to have had a religious experience, is this any more or less likely to be true than someone who claims to have seen a flying saucer? Why?

c) If someone claims to have been told by God in a graveyard to murder young women, might this claim be true? Why?

d) "If one cannot prove that God exists, one should give up belief in God." Do you consider this statement to be fair? Give your reasons.

Ch. 12. Omnipotence
a) If God is all powerful, why does He not stop evil and suffering?

b) Could God commit suicide?

c) Could God make a stone too heavy for Him to lift – and then go on to lift it?

Ch. 13. Omniscience
a) If God knows what we shall do in the future, can we be free?

b) If God knew the suffering and hurt men and women would inflict on each other, was the book of Genesis right to record God as saying that the whole of creation was good?

c) If there is no creator God, in what way might it make sense for a believer to talk of God being omniscient?

Ch. 14. God's Action in the World
a) Do you think that a timeless God could act in the world?

b) If God acts through human beings through the principle of double agency, could human beings still be free?

c) What might an anti-realist mean if she refers to an act of God?

Ch. 15. Petitionary Prayer
a) If a believer prays for those without food in the third world, what is he or she doing?

b) If there is a God who sometimes acts in response to prayer, could such selective action ever be morally justifiable?

c) "Ask and it shall be given to you, seek and you shall find, knock and it shall be opened unto you." What do you think this means?

Ch. 16. Praying for Forgiveness

a) Does it make any difference whether there is or is not a creator God to what a believer is doing when he or she prays for forgiveness?

b) Is it necessary for a priest to have any particular role in prayer for forgiveness? If so, why?

c) "In praying for forgiveness we seek to come to terms with our failings, and to orientate ourselves once more towards human wholeness." Do you consider this a satisfactory definition? Give reasons.

Ch. 17. Miracles

a) Do you think God ever acts directly to bring about events in the world which would not otherwise have happened?

b) Does something being a miracle depend entirely on the way it is seen by believers?

c) If someone you love becomes seriously ill from an incurable disease, would you hope or pray for a miracle? Give your reasons and explain what you would hope for.

Ch. 18. Eternal Life

a) Do you think you will survive death? If so, in what form will you survive?

b) If you will survive death, how would you know if

whatever it is that survives is you rather than a replica of you?

c) Can one experience eternal life in this life? If so, what would it mean?

Ch. 19. And so . . . ?

a) What do you think happened on Easter Sunday? Did Jesus rise from the dead as an individual?

b) Which view of God do you consider to be most plausible?

c) Do you consider that religious people should only believe what they can understand, or what can be rationally justified?

Suggested Further Reading

The following books are suggested for further reading:

Arguments for the existence of God:

Richard Swinburne	—	The Existence of God (Oxford 1979)
J. L. Mackie	—	The Miracle of Theism (Oxford 1982)
J. C. A. Gaskin	—	The Quest for Eternity (Penguin 1984)
David Hume	—	Dialogues concerning Natural Religion
J. Mill	—	Three essays on religion
John Hick	—	The Existence of God (Macmillan 1974)

Religious experience:

Nicholas Lash	—	Easter in ordinary (SCM Press)
William James	—	Varieties of Religious Experience (Fount)
Caroline Davis	—	The evidential force of religious experience (Oxford 1989)

Introduction to Aquinas and to the Thomist approach:

F. Copleston SJ	—	Aquinas (Search Press 1976)
Brian Davies OP	—	Thinking about God
Anthony Kenny	—	Aquinas: A selection of critical essays (Doubleday 1969)

Suggested Further Reading

The realist revisionary view of religious language:

S. Sutherland — God, Jesus and Belief (Blackwell 1983)

The anti-realist revisionary view of religions language:

D. Z. Phillips — Faith after Foundationalism (Routledge 1988)

Gareth Moore OP — Believing in God, a philosophic essay (T. & T. Clarke 1989)

Don Cupitt — The Long Legged fly (SCM 1987)
Taking leave of God (SCM 1980)

Scott Cowdell — Atheist Priest (SCM 1988)

Prayer:

D. Z. Phillips — The Concept of Prayer

V. Brummer — What are we doing when we pray? (SPCK 1984)

C. S. Lewis — Letters to Malcolm (Fount 1966)

Miracles and God's action in the world:

M. Wiles — God's Action in the World (SCM 1986)

Richard Swinburne — The concept of miracle

N. Pike — God and timelessness (Schocken, NY 1970)

T. V. Morris — The Concept of God (section by Stump & Kretzmann)

S. Sutherland — Atheism and the rejection of belief (Blackwell 1977)

Eternal life:

D. Z. Phillips — Death and Immortality (Macmillan 1970)

John Hick	—	Death and Eternal Life (Collins 1976)
Gilbert Ryle	—	The Concept of Mind (Penguin 1970) (classic argument against the dualist position)
Karl Rahner	—	The Theology of Death (Nelson 1961)
John Donnelly	—	Language, Metaphysics and Death (Fordham UP. Series of articles covering related topics.)

Omnipotence and omniscience

T. V. Morris	—	The Concept of God. Chapters with these headings (Oxford 1987)
Boethius	—	The Consolation of Philosophy. Trans. V. Watts (Penguin 1969)
R. H. Nash	—	The Concept of God (Zondervan 1983)
Anthony Kenny	—	The God of the Philosophers (Oxford 1979)
W. L. Craig	—	The Only Wise God (Baker 1987)

The failure of philosophy to understand religious belief:

Peter Vardy	—	And if it's True? (Marshall Pickering)
S. Kierkegaard	—	Fear and Trembling (Penguin)
S. Kierkegaard	—	Training in Christianity (Princeton)